Dear Fellow Member:

Please accept this book as a gift from Radio Bible Class. I am happy to send it to you as my way of saying "thank you" for your support of this ministry.

Written by Paul Van Gorder, associate teacher of the Class, this book is both a survey of the Old Testament and a study of the types of Christ. As you read it, your understanding of the continuity of the entire Bible should be strengthened.

You have been a source of help to us through your prayers and financial support, and I trust that this book will be helpful to you.

Again, thank you, and may God's richest spiritual blessings be yours.

Richard W. DeHaan

Teacher, Radio Bible Class

The Old Testament Presents...

Reflections of Christ

by Paul R. Van Gorder

CONTENTS

Genesis 7

Exodus. 13

Leviticus. 20

Numbers 28

Deuteronomy 34

Joshua 39

Judges 45

Ruth. 50

1 Samuel 56

2 Samuel 60

1 Kings. 65

2 Kings. 70

1 Chronicles 75

2 Chronicles 80

Ezra 83

Nehemiah 87

Esther 92

Job 96

Psalms. 100

Proverbs 105

Ecclesiastes 109

Song of Solomon. . . 114

Isaiah. 119

Jeremiah. 124

Lamentations. 130

Ezekiel. 135

Daniel 140

Hosea 146

Joel. 151

Amos 156

Obadiah. 160

Jonah 163

Micah. 167

Nahum. 171

Habakkuk. 175

Zephaniah. 180

Haggai. 184

Zechariah 188

Malachi 193

PREFACE

With no claim for originality, I have endeavored to peruse the pages of the Old Testament and see there the glorious person and redemptive work of Jesus Christ.

What warrant, you may ask, do I have for attempting to find Him in the pages of the Old Testament? I do so in the light of our Lord's own declaration, "Search the scriptures; for in them ye think ye have eternal life; and they are they which testify of Me" (John 5:39). We heed the example He set when He talked with those disciples walking toward Emmaus: "And beginning at Moses and all the prophets, He expounded unto them, in all the scriptures, the things concerning Himself" (Luke 24:27).

Adolph Saphir wrote: "All attempts to understand Jesus Christ, separate from the Old Testament, are most unphilosophical, and can [produce] no satisfactory result. For Jesus Christ is the fulfillment of Moses and the prophets."

In the course of these studies I will suggest the main themes of each book, outlines of truth, and summaries of content. My intent is that you not only read these chapters but that you study them along with your Bible. This will solidly establish the truth of our Lord's person and work in your heart and life.

On the last pages of this book there is space to write down the pictures of Christ you find in the Old Testament that I have not included. I pray that this volume will serve as a workbook, providing springboards for further study and growth.

Paul R. Van Gorder

GENESIS

Genesis is the seedplot of the Bible. Called by the Jews *bereshith* and by the translators of the Septuagint version "generation," the book gives us the only true history of the origin and early life of man. In it are the seed-principles of all subsequent revelation. Genesis centers about seven prominent persons in pairs. First, Adam and Eve; second, Cain and Abel; third, Enoch and Noah; fourth, Abraham and Lot; fifth, Ishmael and Isaac; sixth, Esau and Jacob; and seventh, Joseph and his brethren.

The book of Genesis can be outlined according to persons, divisions, dispensations, and covenants. I will use a very simple outline based upon the following words: (1) generation, (2) degeneration, and (3) regeneration.

GENERATION (chapters 1 and 2)

This book written by Moses has scriptural proof of its authenticity in the corroborating words of our Lord. Repeatedly Christ quoted from Genesis with the words, "Moses wrote of Me," "Have ye not read in the book of Moses," or "For Moses said."

It is interesting to note that Genesis contains the basic truth of five great sciences:

7

1. *Theology,* the science of God. "In the beginning God created the heaven and the earth" (1:1). "And God said, let *Us* make man in *Our* image" (v. 26). Elohim, the name used for God in Genesis 1:1, is a uni-plural noun. The plural pronoun "us" is followed by the verbs "created" and "said" in the singular. This term expresses both the person and the eternality of God.

2. *Cosmogony,* the science of the universe. "God created the heaven and the earth." Genesis declares that the whole universe came into being by the will and act of God.

3. *Anthropology,* the science of man. The book of Genesis teaches that man was made by the creative act of God. He did not evolve, as modern theory proposes.

4. *Sociology,* the science of society. Genesis tells of the formation of the first societal unit, the family, based upon the marriage relationship. Genesis records the enlarging of the circle of sociology into nations.

5. *Ethnology,* the science of the races. The book of beginnings gives a record of the origin, division, and development of the races of man.

A number of other cardinal doctrines have their roots in the book of Genesis. This leads to the second division of the book.

DEGENERATION (chapters 3-11)

The germ truth of the doctrine of sin, called hamartiology, is found in Genesis. Here we are introduced to Satan, the one who first rebelled. His entire character is infiltrated with subtlety and deceit, and he successfully tempted our first parents. Adam's sin resulted in the murder of Abel by his brother Cain, and the rivulet of iniquity soon became a torrent. The climax of man's sin and rebellion was reached at Calvary, for the biblical record tells us, "For of a truth against Thy holy child, Jesus, whom Thou hast anointed, both Herod, and Pontius Pilate, with the nations, and the people of Israel, were gathered together" (Acts 4:27).

Now, let's look at the third division of the book of Genesis.

REGENERATION (chapters 12-50)

In the seedplot of the Scriptures, Genesis, is found the beginning of soteriology, the doctrine of salvation. In fact, Genesis introduces us to this subject, which is found in all 66 books. The scenario opens in Genesis with the story of sin and death entering God's world; it closes in the last book, Revelation, with the portrayal of the new heavens and new earth in which no trace of evil can be found.

The story of salvation in Genesis is found under two headings: prophecy and types.

1. *Prophecy.* The first prophetic utterance of time is Genesis 3:15, and it foretells the coming of Christ the Redeemer and His victory over Satan. The writer to the Hebrews said, "Forasmuch, then, as the children are partakers of flesh and blood, He also Himself likewise took part of the same, that through death He might destroy him that had the power of death, that is, the devil" (Hebrews 2:14).

Jehovah made this promise to Abraham: "In thee shall all families of the earth be blessed" (Genesis 12:3). To Jacob, God said, "And I will make thy seed to multiply as the stars of heaven, and will give unto thy seed all these countries; and in thy seed shall all the nations of the earth be blessed" (Genesis 26:4). And in a prophetic blessing to Judah, Jacob predicted, "The scepter shall not depart from Judah, nor a lawgiver from between his feet, until Shiloh come; and unto Him shall the gathering of the people be" (Genesis 49:10). The fulfillment of these prophecies is recorded in Luke 1:32 and Revelation 5.

2. *Types.* In his first epistle, Simon Peter declared that the prophets who spoke of the grace that should come searched "what manner of time the Spirit of Christ who was in them did signify, when He testified beforehand the sufferings of Christ, and the glory that should follow" (1 Peter 1:11). And where in Genesis do we find the Lord Jesus Christ pictured, both His sufferings and His glory? With your Bible opened and notebook and pen in hand, I suggest to you the following

possibilities, and urge that you study the Scripture passages carefully.

Christ, the Sun of righteousness (Genesis 1:16). The Lord Jesus said, "I am the light of the world" (John 8:12). The prophet Malachi spoke about the "Sun of righteousness" that shall arise (4:2). So, Christ is represented by the sun; the church is the lesser light reflecting the light of the sun.

Christ, the last Adam, the second man. He is typified by the first man, Adam, in contrast. Adam was the head of the old creation; Christ is the head of the new. (See 1 Corinthians 15:22, 45-47; Romans 5:12-19.)

Christ, the bridegroom of the church (see Genesis 2:18-24). God's provision of a helper suitable for Adam is a picture of what was accomplished at Calvary. When the deep sleep of death came upon our Lord, and from His riven side poured forth blood and water, the picture was complete. Christ "loved the church, and gave Himself for it" (Ephesians 5:25).

Christ, the righteousness of God (Genesis 3:21). In the Bible a garment is often the symbol of righteousness. We read in Isaiah 61:10, "For He hath clothed Me with the garments of salvation, He hath covered Me with the robe of righteousness . . . ." First Corinthians 1:30 states, "But of Him are ye in Christ Jesus, who of God is made unto us wisdom, and righteousness, and sanctification, and redemption." In Eden, an innocent animal had to be sacrificed before the "coats of skins" were provided.

Christ, the Lamb of God (Genesis 4:4). Abel's offering of a slain lamb stands in direct contrast with Cain's bloodless offering. "Without shedding of blood is no remission" (Hebrews 9:22). That lamb, the firstling of the flock, portrayed the innocence and harmlessness of an obedient Christ (read Isaiah 53:7).

Christ, our refuge from judgment. Look at Genesis 7:1 and 8:1, then read the New Testament commentary in Hebrews 11:7. The picture of Christ as our protector is especially applicable to the remnant of Israel during the great tribulation (Matthew 24:21,22). Enoch is a type of the church, for he had already been taken out of the world prior to the flood of judgment. Noah and his family are types of Israel, for they were preserved through the flood. The word "pitch" of Genesis 6:14 is the word translated "atonement" in Leviticus 17:11.

Christ, the high priest after the order of Melchizedek (Genesis 14:18-20). The words "after the order of Melchizedek" refer to the unending priesthood of our Savior (read Hebrews 7).

Christ, the obedient Son and willing sacrifice (Genesis 21). How beautifully this truth is typified by Isaac! Isaac's life was ordered by his father. Similarly, the Lord Jesus said, "I seek not Mine own will, but the will of the Father who hath sent Me" (John 5:30). Christ was portrayed by Isaac in the following elements:

- Isaac was the promised seed (Genesis 15:4).
- He became obedient unto death (22:9).
- He was raised from the dead in a figure (22:12,13).
- He received a Gentile bride (24).

Christ, typified by Joseph. Ada Habershon, in the book *The Study of the Types,* actually lists over 100 fore-shadowings of Christ as seen in Joseph. Here are a few for your personal study:

1. Beloved of his father (Genesis 37:3).
2. Hated and rejected by his brethren (37:4).
3. Brothers plot to slay him, and figuratively they do so (37:20-27).
4. Lifted up out of the pit (37:28).
5. Went to the Gentiles; received and favored (39:1-6).
6. Received a Gentile bride during his rejection (41:45).
7. Reconciled to his brethren; and they are blessed through him (45).

Who can plumb the depths of the great types and analogies given to us in the book of Genesis? For your personal study, I would suggest similar possibilities in Eve, Enoch, Rebekah, and the theophanies (the pre-incarnate appearings of the Lord Jesus), such as occurred on the plains of Mamre recorded in Genesis 18.

The book of Genesis begins with the creation by God: "In the beginning God . . . ." It ends with a coffin in Egypt (50:26). At the very beginning of the human race we see the sad failure of man and the gracious provision of God. The first great promise of a coming Redeemer is found in Genesis 3:15. That promise leaps the centuries and finds its fulfillment in the death and resurrection of the Lord Jesus Christ, the seed of the woman.

Genesis is indeed the seedplot of the entire Bible!

EXODUS

The overriding theme of the book of Exodus is redemption. The Hebrew title of this book is translated, "these are the names." This is in perfect harmony with the subject of the book, for redemption is an *individual* matter. The word "exodus" comes from the title in the Septuagint version, and means literally, "going out."

Israel had been in Egypt for 400 years in bondage and slavery. God remembered them, raised up Moses as a deliverer, and brought them out of the land of Egypt. This book records the redemption of Israel from bondage, and it is typical of all redemption. Redemption is:

1. *Totally of God.* Israel was helpless. Pharaoh represents Satan and the bondage he inflicts. Egypt pictures the world.

2. *Through a person.* Moses, Israel's deliverer, pictures the Lord Jesus Christ, our Deliverer.

3. *By blood.* The apostle Peter wrote, "Forasmuch as ye know that ye were not redeemed with corruptible things, like silver and gold, from your vain manner of life received by tradition from your fathers, but with the precious blood of Christ, as of a lamb without blemish and without spot" (1 Peter 1:18,19).

4. *By power.* God demonstrated His power in putting a difference between the people of Egypt and the people of Israel (Exodus 11:7). By His mighty arm He brought Israel out of Egypt and through the Red Sea (see Exodus 14:21,22; Romans 3:25,26).

OUTLINE OF THE BOOK

I. History
   A. Slavery (1-14)
   B. Emancipation (15-18)
   C. Reconstruction (19-40)

II. Geography
   A. Egypt (1-13)
   B. Red Sea (14)
   C. Sinai (15-40)

III. Time
   A. Moses' 40 years in the palace of Pharaoh (1:1-2:14)
   B. His 40 years of preparation in the desert (2:15-4)
   C. His 40 years of service with the nation Israel (5-40)

PROPHETIC PICTURES OF CHRIST

If the theme of Exodus is redemption, then the book must be filled with foreshadowings of Christ and His work. We will look at five specific prophetic pictures in detail. We will also consider the life and ministry of Moses and Aaron and see them as types of our Lord Jesus Christ.

The Burning Bush. Exodus 3 contains the account of the burning bush and the call of Moses. This was a common little thorn bush, and Moses no doubt had seen many of them in the desert. This one looked like all the other bushes, yet it was different. The little acacia shrub burned, but it was not consumed. A voice coming out of the bush said, "I AM THAT I AM" (v. 14). Only an eternal, self-existent, immutable Being could say that He always will be what He always has been. Centuries later, One stood upon the earth as a man. He was born in Bethlehem, was brought up in a carpenter's shop, and was tempted in every way we are without ever sinning. We hear Him say, "I AM the door, I AM the bread of life, I AM the light of the world, I AM the good shepherd, I AM the way, the truth, and the life, I AM the true vine—I AM!" John wrote, "The Word was made flesh, and dwelt among us (and we beheld His glory, the glory as of the only begotten of the Father), full of grace and truth" (John 1:14). The One born in that human body in Bethlehem was God manifest in the flesh. He was made in the likeness of man, yet He was aglow with deity. Only He could dare say to the Father, "Glorify Thou Me with Thine own self with the glory which I had with Thee before the world was" (John 17:5).

The Passover Lamb. Israel was enslaved by a powerful monarch in Egypt. How was God to get them out and yet execute His justice, maintain His holiness, and show His love and mercy? Exodus 12 tells the story. He accomplished their release through the blood of the passover lamb. First Corinthians 5:7 states unequivocally, "For even Christ, our passover, is sacrificed for us." How beautifully that paschal lamb portrayed the death of God's Lamb, the Lord Jesus!

1. *The lamb was a male, a firstling of the flock, and without blemish* (Exodus 12:5). We are redeemed "with the precious blood of Christ, as of a lamb without blemish and without spot" (1 Peter 1:19).

2. *The lamb was kept 4 days for examination* (Exodus 12:3-6). What scrutiny our Lord came under by friend and foe! Only He could say, "Which of you convicteth Me of sin?" (John 8:46).

3. *The lamb must be slain* (Exodus 12:6). Christ said of Himself, "Verily, verily, I say unto you, Except a grain of wheat fall into the ground and die, it abideth alone; but if it die, it bringeth forth much fruit" (John 12:24). It was not His life as an example nor His words as a teacher but the shedding of His blood as the perfect sacrifice that secured our redemption.

4. *The blood had to be applied* (Exodus 12:7). Read

15

John 3:36, which says, "He that believeth on the Son hath everlasting life; and he that believeth not the Son shall not see life, but the wrath of God abideth on him."

5. *The blood was applied and that alone brought salvation* (Exodus 12:23). The writer of Hebrews said, "By which will we are sanctified through the offering of the body of Jesus Christ once for all. For by one offering He hath perfected forever them that are sanctified" (Hebrews 10:10,14).

6. *Not a bone of the passover lamb was to be broken* (Exodus 12:46). Consider the account of Christ's crucifixion and the record of John 19:33. "But when they came to Jesus, and saw that He was dead already, they broke not His legs."

7. *Sheltered by the blood, they were nourished by the roast lamb.* This typified Christ as the believer's sustenance and food (see Matthew 26:26).

How does a mother bird protect her nest? Not by flying by it, but by fluttering over it. That night in Egypt, Jehovah Himself stood guard over (literally, hovered over) the houses of Israel where the blood had been applied and kept their firstborn safe from death.

The Manna. When redeemed Israel was marching toward Canaan, God gave them manna, food from heaven. In John 6 the Lord Jesus said, "My Father giveth you the true bread from heaven. I am the bread of life; he that cometh to Me shall never hunger" (John 6:32,35). Consider the amazing analogy between the manna and the Lord Jesus Christ! The manna came down from heaven; it was a gift of God; men tried to explain it naturally; it was given at night; it was sent when Israel was about to perish; it came to the place they were; it was gathered only by stooping; it had to be gathered individually; either they gathered it or walked upon it; it was despised by the mixed multitude; it was mysterious to Israel; it was preserved over the Sabbath day; it was laid up before Jehovah; it met the daily need; and it was eventually hidden in the ark.

The Water from the Rock. Exodus 17 records the experience of the people of Israel at Rephidim, where "there was no water for the people to drink" (v. 1). God commanded Moses to smite the rock, and water gushed forth. That smitten rock was a type of Christ, as we are told in 1 Corinthians 10:4. The people were murmuring and complaining and were totally unworthy of this act of grace (read Ephesians 2:1-8). God's grace is free, abundant (Romans 5:20), near (Romans 10:8), and available to all who will take it (Isaiah 55:1). The water gushing forth pictured the Spirit given freely (John 7:37-40). The people of Israel could not drink of the refreshing water until the rock was first smitten. Before the Holy Spirit could be given, Christ had to die at Calvary.

To a sinning, murmuring people God had displayed His grace. It was as Paul said in Romans 5:20, "But where sin abounded, grace did much more abound."

Tabernacle and Priesthood. While only two chapters in Genesis are occupied with the creation of the world, fourteen chapters in Exodus are taken up with the tabernacle. This shows the esteem God places upon the work of redemption, and that Christ is the center and object of the Spirit's revelation. For your further study, I mention the following elements of the tabernacle that graphically portray the way of approach to God.
1. The entire tabernacle was a figure of the heavenly (Hebrews 9:23,24).
2. The ark of the covenant.
   a. Acacia wood and gold: the humanity and deity of Christ.
   b. Contents of the ark: a type of Christ.
      The law: Christ had God's law in His heart; He was the fulfillment of the law.
      Manna: Christ is sustenance to believers on their pilgrimage.
      Aaron's rod: Christ's resurrection.
   c. The ark: A type of the throne of grace; the mercy seat: the Lord Jesus.
3. The table of showbread: Christ our communion.
4. The candlestick: Christ our light (Hebrews 1:9; Revelation 1:9-18).

5. The altar of incense: Christ our advocate
   and intercessor.
6. The laver: the cleansing by the Word and
   by Christ.
7. Bronze altar: the cross of Christ and
   His atonement.
8. Anointing oil: the Holy Spirit's anointing
   for service.
9. Garments: gold for righteousness; blue for
   heavenly; purple for royalty; scarlet
   for sacrifice.

The writer of Hebrews said, "And they, truly, were many priests, because they were not allowed to continue by reason of death; but this man, because He continueth ever, hath an unchangeable priesthood. Wherefore, He is able also to save them to the uttermost that come unto God by Him, seeing He ever liveth to make intercession for them" (Hebrews 7:23-25). Aaron fell short in his priesthood because he was a sinful man and subject to death. The type is therefore seen in contrast. Christ is able to understand our need to the uttermost because He is a perfect man. He is able to meet all our need because He is God. At the cross He was qualified to bear the whole world's sin in His atonement. At the throne He is able to care for our need through His intercession.

Christ is "a priest forever after the order of Melchizedek" in that He is our intercessor forever. But His priesthood is after the pattern of Aaron. First, Aaron was appointed by God (Exodus 28:1). We read in Hebrews 5:5, "So also Christ glorified not Himself to be made an high priest, but He that said unto Him, Thou art My Son, today have I begotten Thee." Second, only Aaron could make atonement in the holy place (Leviticus 16:1-3). Of our Lord it is written, "Neither by the blood of goats and calves, but by His own blood He entered in once into the holy place, having obtained eternal redemption for us" (Hebrews 9:12).

THE GREAT QUESTION
How is it possible for a holy God to receive sinners with-

18

out violating His righteousness and justice? The inspired answer comes from the book of Exodus: "When I see the blood, I will pass over you" (12:13). Sin was judged, and the blood was shed; Israel was saved and received.

LEVITICUS

This book derives its name from "Levi," the priestly tribe chosen by God to carry on the tabernacle service. Leviticus, the book of worship, work, and walk, naturally follows Exodus, the book of redemption.

The key word of Leviticus, "holiness," is used 87 times. The key verse is: "Ye shall be holy; for I, the Lord your God, am holy" (Leviticus 19:2).

In the Hebrew Bible this book is called *vayikra*, meaning, "and He called." The book consists almost entirely of words spoken by Jehovah from the tabernacle. Sacrifice is the basis of approach to God; priesthood is the means of access. Every offering, every drop of blood speaks of the One who is made unto us wisdom, righteousness, sanctification, and redemption.

OUTLINE OF THE BOOK
    I. Sacrifice (1-6:7)
   II. The Law of the Offerings (6:8-7)
  III. Consecration (8-9)
   IV. A Warning Example (10)
    V. A Holy God Demands a Clean People (11-15)
   VI. Atonement (16,17)

VII. Relationships of God's People (18-22)
VIII. The Feasts of Jehovah (23)
  IX. Instructions and Warnings (24-27)

Few of the Old Testament books reflect Christ more than Leviticus. Over every offering, ceremony, feast, garment, utensil, and article (except leaven), you may write the word "Christ." Let's focus briefly on how the offerings and the feasts portray the Lord Jesus.

THE OFFERINGS

Two types of offerings are specified in Leviticus: (1) the sweet-savor offerings demonstrate that Christ was acceptable to God; (2) the nonsweet-savor offerings demonstrate that the sinner is unacceptable, but that God's justice fell upon Christ as He became the sinner's substitute. The sweet-savor offerings are Godward; the nonsweet-savor offerings are manward.

The Burnt Offering (chapter 1). This was a sweet-savor offering (see Philippians 2:8). The burnt sacrifice was to be a male animal without blemish, portraying the One "who through the eternal Spirit offered Himself without spot to God" (Hebrews 9:14). It was to be made voluntarily. Our Lord said, "No man taketh it [life] from Me, but I lay it down of Myself" (John 10:18). Every detail of the sacrifice was ordered by God. It was laid in order upon the wood. The offering was flayed and cut in pieces, exposing the inner flesh. The inward parts and legs of the animal were washed with water, which speak of the motives and walk of the believer, his manner of life. Our Lord could say, "I do always those things that please Him [the Father]" (John 8:29). The sacrifice, the burnt offering, was substitutionary, for "it shall be accepted for him" (Leviticus 1:4). The offerer put his hand upon the animal to identify himself with it. So also Christ "hath loved us, and hath given Himself for us an offering and a sacrifice to God for a sweet-smelling savor" (Ephesians 5:2).

The Meat (or Meal) Offering (chapter 2). This was another sweet-savor offering, and it pictured the perfect person and character of Christ. It consisted of

21

finely ground flour with no lumps in it. Jesus Christ displayed no unevenness in His humanity. Oil, symbol of the Holy Spirit, was then poured out upon the fine flour. The Heavenly Father anointed the Lord Jesus with the Holy Spirit. Then frankincense was placed upon the oil and flour. This gave forth a fragrance when fire was applied. Our Lord stated in John 4:34 "My food is to do the will of Him that sent Me, and to finish His work." His death completed the picture.

In addition to the above, the sacrifice was seasoned with salt. Salt is a barrier against corruption. This word is sometimes used in Scripture in connection with speech. Colossians 4:6 says, "Let your speech be always with grace, seasoned with salt." The believer is told, "Let the word of Christ dwell in you richly" (Colossians 3:16). And they said of our Lord, "Never man spoke like this man" (John 7:46).

There was to be no leaven in the sweet-savor offering of fine flour. Christ was "holy, harmless, undefiled, separate from sinners" (Hebrews 7:26). Furthermore, no honey was to be used in the offering, for honey is a symbol of nature's sweetness. The offering, made by fire unto the Lord, typifies the perfect man, Christ Jesus, enduring the fire of judgment.

A handful of this offering of flour, oil, and frankincense was presented to God. The rest was eaten by the priests. How beautifully this pictures our spiritual nourishment as we partake of Christ, our meal offering, who was sacrificed for us! We abide in Him, and His words abide in us.

The Peace Offering (chapter 3). The law of this offering is found in Leviticus 7:28-36. It presents a beautiful picture of reconciliation, making possible communion with God. This offering was made by fire because it took judgment to bring peace. The offerer was to "lay his hand upon the head of his offering and kill it at the door of the tabernacle of the congregation" (3:2). Then Aaron's sons, the priests, sprinkled the blood upon the altar. The New Testament fulfillment says, "And, having made peace through the blood of His cross, by Him to reconcile all things unto Himself" (Colossians 1:20).

Once the reconciliation was accomplished by the sprinkling of the blood, the priests were to eat of the sacrifice (7:32-34). This speaks of communion and fellowship. The priests and the ones presenting the peace offering both ate of it in the presence of the Lord. This sacrifice was the basis of their peace and fellowship. It was indeed a "thank offering" (7:11,12).

The Sin Offering (chapter 4). This offering, not a sweet-savor offering, stands in contrast with the burnt offering. The burnt offering was all for God; the sin offering was all for man. In the burnt offering the believer is seen as identified with Christ. In the sin offering, Christ is seen as identified with the believer's sin. These factors apply:

1. It was given for sins of ignorance. Man is a sinner (see Romans 8:3), whether he knows it or not.
2. The victim was to be without blemish. To be our substitute, Christ had to be sinless.
3. The victim was the substitute for the sinner (see 2 Corinthians 5:21).
4. The blood poured out at the bottom of the altar was a picture of the shedding of Christ's blood.
5. The victim was taken outside the camp and burned to ashes. Christ died outside the city wall (Hebrews 13:12; Lamentations 1:12,13).
6. The relation of the offerer to the offering was:
   a. He had to admit that he was a sinner.
   b. He had to accept God's estimate of himself.
   c. He had to identify himself with the substitute.
   d. He had to take the God-provided sacrifice.
7. The relation of the sin offering to the offerer was:
   a. The blood was within the veil, indicating that the sacrifice had been accepted.
   b. The ashes were spread outside the camp, showing sins put away. Christ outside the camp died for us; Christ inside the veil is living for us.

The Trespass Offering (chapter 5). The sin offering was a sacrifice for *the nature of sin.* The trespass offering,

23

another nonsweet-savor offering, was a sacrifice for *the sins of nature.* The sin offering dealt with the root; the trespass offering with the fruit.

The trespass offering was of *expiation;* the guilt of sin was taken away. It was also of *restoration;* that which was lost by the first Adam is restored by the last Adam, the Lord Jesus. It also involved *restitution;* the offerer was to restore to the person that which he had unjustly taken, and he was to add a fifth part to it to compensate for the wrong.

The cleansing from sins was made possible through confession (Leviticus 5:5). Likewise, the Lord Jesus died, not only for what we *are* by nature but also for what we *do* because of that nature. Furthermore, the Christian knows that "if we confess our sins, He is faithful and just to forgive us our sins, and to cleanse us from all unrighteousness" (1 John 1:9). Read also 1 John 2:1.

The levitical offerings began with the burnt offering and ended with the trespass offering. This is the order of God's provision for man, for "salvation is of the Lord." Christians, however, see the meaning of these offerings in just the reverse order.

1. Conviction of sins: the trespass offering.
2. Recognition of the root of these sins: the sin offering.
3. Peace with God: the peace offering.
4. The desire to know more of the wonderful person of Christ: the meal offering.
5. Unswerving devotion to God: the burnt offering.

THE FEASTS OF JEHOVAH

Leviticus 23 outlines the sacred calendar of redemption. These seven feasts in the Jewish year foretell and set forth the plan of salvation from the death of Christ through His millennial reign. They give us in sequence the different stages in God's redemptive scheme.

I suggest that you study carefully the details of each feast named in Leviticus 23, for they are "a shadow of things to come" (Colossians 2:17).

24

The Feast of Passover (vv. 4,5). The history of redemption begins with the passover. To Israel this was the first feast and the beginning of months to them. This feast commemorated their deliverance from Egypt, and 1 Corinthians 5:7 says that "Christ, our passover, is sacrificed for us." There is no way to God apart from the work of Christ upon the cross. We can know nothing of holiness, rest, or fellowship except on redemption ground. And that begins with passover.

The Feast of Unleavened Bread (vv. 6-8). This feast began on the next day after the passover and continued for 7 days. It was closely associated with passover because the Israelites ate the roast lamb and the unleavened bread that night in Egypt (Exodus 12:8). The blood was their foundation of fellowship with God; the feeding upon the lamb was the means of maintaining fellowship. Unleavened bread speaks of holiness, the condition necessary for the enjoyment of fellowship. "For even Christ, our passover, is sacrificed for us. Therefore, let us keep the feast" (1 Corinthians 5:7,8). Fellowship is established on the basis of the applied blood. But fellowship is maintained as we walk in holiness of life, obedient unto God.

The Feast of Firstfruits (vv. 9-14). First Corinthians 15:20 states, "But now is Christ risen from the dead and become the firstfruits of them that slept." The feast of firstfruits represents His resurrection. At the beginning of the harvest, the Israelites cut a sheaf of grain and brought it to the priest, who waved it before the Lord. He did this to show that it was accepted by God on the sinner's behalf (v. 11). Christ's resurrection has been accepted by God for us and is the guarantee of our own.

The Feast of Wave Loaves, or Pentecost (vv. 15-22). This feast took place 50 days after the feast of firstfruits. Its New Testament fulfillment is found in Acts, chapter 2. Fifty days after the resurrection of the Lord Jesus, the Holy Spirit descended upon waiting Jewish believers. Later, the same was experienced in the household of Cornelius, a Gentile. Both Jews and

Gentiles were formed into one body, the church, the body of Christ.

The wave-loaf offering consisted of two loaves baked with leaven. Its counterpart, the church, has in it leaven (evil) because of the old nature of its members. Although evil is present, it has been taken care of by a burnt offering, a sin offering, and a peace offering.

This feast therefore pictures the Holy Spirit's descent at Pentecost to bind the waiting believers into one body.

The Feast of Trumpets (vv. 23-25). This event was observed on the first day of the seventh month. A long interval of 4 months stood between the feast of pentecost and the feast of trumpets. This interval corresponds to the present church age. There were always two trumpets in Israel: one for assembly and another for war. First Corinthians 15:52 says, "The trumpet shall sound, and the dead shall be raised incorruptible." Likewise, Matthew 24:31 states, "He shall send His angels with a great sound of a trumpet, and they shall gather together His elect." One trumpet sounds for the rapture of the church; another trumpet sounds later for the gathering of Israel. Please read and compare Isaiah 18:3,4; Isaiah 27:12,13; Joel 2:15-17.

The Day of Atonement (vv. 26-32). This feast closely followed the feast of trumpets, occurring on the tenth day of the seventh month. The sacrifices of that day included a sin offering and a burnt offering for Aaron and his house; and two goats for a sin offering and a ram for a burnt offering for the congregation. The blood of the slain goat, sprinkled within the veil, pictures the setting of the claims of God's justice. The live goat that was led away into the wilderness pictures our Lord bearing away our sins.

Three characteristics were evident in the celebration of atonement: first, affliction of soul (Zechariah 12:10-14; Jeremiah 8:20); second, atonement for sin (Zechariah 13:1); and third, rest from labor. Just as the day of atonement closed with the appearance of the high priest from behind the veil, so Israel's future day of atonement will be climaxed with the appearance of their Messiah, the Lord Jesus Christ, from heaven.

The Feast of Tabernacles (vv. 33-44). The time setting for this feast is given in Deuteronomy 16:13, "After thou hast gathered in thy grain and thy wine." The fruit of the field and the vintage of the earth—after these two are harvested, this feast is celebrated. The feast speaks of the millennial reign of Christ. There will be a time of rejoicing over a regathered and redeemed Israel. (Be sure to read of that important time in Zechariah 14:16-21). Life's battles will finally be over. Sword and spear will be changed into instruments of peace. Every man will sit under his own vine and fig tree, enjoying a balanced economy (Micah 4:4). Earth's glorious sabbath of 1,000 years will have begun.

Throughout the book of Leviticus we are given glimpses of the holiness that is ours as God's redeemed, the holiness that becomes ours through a life of obedience, and the perfect holiness that will be ours in the millennial age to come.

NUMBERS

The book of Numbers records the wilderness journey-
ings of the children of Israel. A key phrase of the book,
"all who were able to go forth to war," appears 14 times
in chapter one. In typology, the theme of Numbers is
service and walk.

The location of this book in the Pentateuch is of considerable significance. Genesis speaks of creation and
fall. Exodus tells the story of redemption. Leviticus is
the book of worship and fellowship. And Numbers
focuses upon service and walk. This is the Divine order;
the order in the life of a Christian. Sad to say, Numbers
does not give the record of a holy, sanctified walk by
Israel. In fact, it might better be called "the book of
murmurings." Instead of marching into Canaan within
a few weeks of leaving Egypt, the Israelites wandered
in the wilderness for 40 years.

OUTLINE OF THE BOOK

     I. Sinai to Kadesh-barnea (1-12)
    II. Rebellion at Kadesh-barnea and 38 Years
       of Wandering (13-33)
   III. Return to Kadesh-barnea and Related
       Events (34-36)

Let us now turn to an analysis of the major themes of
the book of Numbers as they relate to our overall purpose, a study of Christ in the Old Testament.

THE NUMBERING OF ISRAEL (chapters 1-9)

The way the camp of Israel was arranged was significant. The tabernacle was in the center, and three tribes were located on each side of the tabernacle. Remember, the tabernacle and its furnishings speak graphically of Christ and His work.

After Adam and Eve were expelled from the garden of Eden, cherubim guarded the way to the tree of life (Genesis 3:24). A representation of these cherubim was attached to the mercy seat over the ark of the covenant. In Ezekiel chapters 1 and 10 we read again of these same living creatures. Finally, we see them in the Revelation. The cherubim have the face of a *lion*, the face of an *ox*, the face of a *man*, and the face of an *eagle*.

On the east of the tabernacle, three tribes were located with Judah as the standard bearer, *the lion*. On the west side were three tribes with Ephraim as standard bearer, *the ox*. On the south, three tribes camped with Reuben as standard bearer, *the man*. The three remaining tribes were located on the north with Dan as standard bearer, *the eagle*. This may well speak of Christ as pictured in the four gospels: king (lion), servant (ox), man, and God (eagle).

As you read the first nine chapters of Numbers and observe the minuteness of every detail, you will learn that every tribe and every family had its own work and carried it out. How wonderful if the church, the body of Christ, would be as faithful!

THE NAZIRITE (chapter 6)

A Nazirite was a lay person who was bound by a vow of consecration to God's service. Certain practices characterized the Nazirite. First, he did not touch wine. The fruit of the vine in the Bible is often the symbol of *natural* joy. The joy of our Lord, however, was *supernatural*. Second, the Nazirite never allowed a razor or shears to touch his hair. His unshorn hair demonstrated that he had taken the position of weakness (1 Corinthians 11:14). We read in Philippians 2:7,8 that our Lord "made Himself of no reputation, and took upon Him the form of a servant, and was made in the likeness of men; and, being found in fashion as a man, He humbled Himself."

And another passage says, "For though He was crucified through weakness, yet He liveth by the power of God" (2 Corinthians 13:4). Third, the Nazirite kept himself from defilement, even while among good people. Similar circumstances in the life of the Lord Jesus are indicated in Matthew 12:47-50.

THE CLOUD (chapter 9)

After the Israelites were all numbered, in place, and ready to go forward, then the cloud would lift and they would march (Numbers 9:15-19). Whenever the cloud settled, they camped. The pillar of fire by night and the cloud by day indicated God's leading by His presence.

Similarly, the believer has the word of Christ. "I am the light of the world; he that followeth Me shall not walk in darkness, but shall have the light of life" (John 8:12). Not only did Israel have the pillar of cloud by day but also a pillar of fire by night. The Holy Spirit, our "fire," has come down to "guide [us] into all truth" (John 16:13). The Christian may joyfully sing with the poet, "He leadeth me! O blessed thought! / O words with heavenly comfort fraught! / Whate'er I do, wher-e'er I be, / Still 'tis God's hand that leadeth me."

AARON'S ROD THAT BUDDED (chapters 16,17)

A rebellion arose within Israel, led by Korah, Dathan, and Abiram; they wanted to usurp the office of the priesthood. They hurled the accusation that "ye take too much upon you" (16:3) against Moses and Aaron. The judgment of God fell upon them and the earth swallowed them up. Then the children of Israel, the congregation, gathered against Moses and Aaron and murmured because of the death of these rebels.

God validated the priesthood of Aaron by having the princes of each of the tribes come with a rod. The name of each prince was inscribed upon the rod, and Aaron's name was inscribed upon that of Levi. The 12 rods were spread out before the ark of the covenant. The next morning only one of those rods had life in it. Aaron's rod had budded, bloomed, and yielded almonds. The hand of God reaffirmed convincingly that Aaron and his family were His choice for the priesthood.

The Lord Jesus Christ has been "declared to be the Son of God with power, according to the spirit of holiness, by the resurrection from the dead" (Romans 1:4). By that resurrection God accepted and designated the Lord Jesus as the ever-living High Priest. The religions of the world can only point to dead leaders, for sepulchers still hold fast the remains of those leaders. Christians alone have a living, interceding High Priest. "Seeing, then, that we have a great high priest, that is passed into the heavens, Jesus, the Son of God, let us hold fast our profession" (Hebrews 4:14).

THE RED HEIFER (chapter 19)

God prescribed for Israel both a basis and method of cleansing. The sacrifice was to be a red heifer that was without blemish or spot and that had never borne a yoke. This speaks of the spotless character of Christ, who never came under the yoke of the curse for sin. That heifer was slain outside the camp. So also our Lord, though holy, was treated as unclean. By this He became the substitute for the unclean.

The entire sacrifice had to be consumed. Christ offered Himself—every part—unto God. Cedar and hyssop and scarlet were cast into the midst of the burning sacrifice. The ashes from the sacrifice were gathered up and laid in a clean place—set apart for those that were defiled. Likewise our Lord went through the agony and sacrifice of Calvary, and His body was laid in a clean, new tomb. But He did not remain there. He arose from the grave, and "He ever liveth to make intercession for us" (Hebrews 7:25).

The Israelites were told, "He who toucheth the dead body of any man shall be unclean seven days" (Numbers 19:11). Just a touch was enough to make a person unclean. Death is the work of sin, and the entire race has come under sin's penalty. "There is none righteous, no, not one" (Romans 3:10). The believer in Jesus, after he has received by faith the sacrifice of Christ, comes in contact with the defilement of the flesh and the world. Just a touch of sin is enough to break fellowship with God and render a person unclean.

For such an unclean person in Israel, the priest sprinkled the ashes of the burnt heifer in running water and put them into a container. Then a clean person would dip hyssop in the water and sprinkle it upon the tent, the utensils, and the person that had become unclean. This speaks of cleansing from the defilement of sin. The slaying of the sacrifice and the keeping of the ashes were not enough. For the sacrifice to be effective, it had to be appropriated through the ceremony of the running water.

How vividly this speaks of the water of the Word! The Lord Jesus said, "Now ye are clean through the word which I have spoken unto you" (John 15:3). Just as it was running water for Israel, so it is by the moving of the Spirit of God through the Word that we are convicted of our sin and also cleansed from it. Paul said that Christ gave Himself for the church "that He might sanctify and cleanse it with the washing of water by the word" (Ephesians 5:26). The apostle John wrote, "But if we walk in the light, as He is in the light, we have fellowship one with another, and the blood of Jesus Christ, His Son, cleanseth us from all sin. If we say that we have no sin, we deceive ourselves, and the truth is not in us. If we confess our sins, He is faithful and just to forgive us our sins, and to cleanse us from all unrighteousness" (1 John 1:7-9).

THE BRONZE SERPENT (chapter 21)

For the eighth time on their wilderness journey, the children of Israel murmured and complained. So God sent fiery serpents among them in judgment. When they were bitten by those snakes, the venom spread throughout their bodies. All across the camp of Israel, people were dying. So God commanded Moses to prepare a bronze serpent that looked like the ones that had bitten the people and place it upon a pole. We know that this bronze serpent was a type of Christ lifted up on the cross and made sin for us, because He said,

And, as Moses lifted up the serpent in the wilderness, even so must the Son of man be lifted up,

That whosoever believeth in Him should not perish, but have eternal life.

For God so loved the world, that He gave His only begotten Son, that whosoever believeth in Him should not perish, but have everlasting life (John 3:14-16).

Note these significant facts:

1. The bronze serpent on the pole was divinely provided. Salvation is of the Lord.
2. It was divinely suitable. Every person who was bitten could look and be healed. The remedy was within reach. "Look unto Me, and be saved, all the ends of the earth" (Isaiah 45:22).
3. It was divinely effectual. Numbers 21 says that anyone who looked would be healed. God did the saving; man simply looked in faith.

THE CITIES OF REFUGE (chapter 35)

The Lord Jesus Christ is also seen in the unique provision recorded in this chapter of Numbers. The cities of refuge were a type of Christ, sheltering the sinner from judgment. They may also be applied to Israel, who slew the Prince of life "through ignorance" (Acts 3:17).

The believing sinner, even though he is guilty, has this promise from God's Word: "There is, therefore, now no condemnation to them who are in Christ Jesus" (Romans 8:1). The writer to the Hebrews said, "That by two immutable things, in which it was impossible for God to lie, we might have a strong consolation, who have fled for refuge to lay hold upon the hope set before us" (Hebrews 6:18).

Yes, my friend, in its pictures of Christ's person and work, the book of Numbers corroborates the statement of our Lord that "they are they which testify of Me" (John 5:39).

DEUTERONOMY

The name "Deuteronomy" means "second law" or "second law-giving." Let's get a picture of the scene. The desert wanderings of Israel are almost over. Moses is near the end of his life. And here on the plains of Moab opposite Jericho, Moses speaks to the children of Israel about their future.

The key words of Deuteronomy are "thou shalt" and "thou shalt not." If we were to write one word across this book to state its theme, it would be "obedience." The significant promise and the ominous warning are seen in Deuteronomy 11:26-28, which sums it all up:

Behold, I set before you this day a blessing and a curse:

A blessing, if ye obey the commandments of the Lord your God, which I command you this day;

And a curse, if ye will not obey the commandments of the Lord your God, but turn aside out of the way which I command you this day, to go after other gods, which ye have not known.

The book of Deuteronomy may be comfortably divided according to the addresses of Moses.

OUTLINE OF THE BOOK

    I. Forty Years of Wandering (1-4)
    II. Promise of Blessings for Obedience and Curses for Disobedience (5-28)
    III. The Palestinian Covenant (29,30)
    IV. Joshua Appointed Moses' Successor (31)
    V. The Farewell Song of Moses (32)
    VI. Final Blessings for the Tribes; Moses' Death (33,34)

SPIRITUAL TEACHING

Deuteronomy shows with unmistakable clarity the inflexibility of the law and the necessity of complete subjection to the Word of God. As Romans 3:19 declares, "Now we know that whatever things the law saith, it saith to them who are under the law, that every mouth may be stopped, and all the world may become guilty before God."

Christ is the fulfillment of the law. He is the only Israelite to obey God totally in the promised land. He alone kept the letter of the code that was set forth in Deuteronomy.

GREATEST VALUE

The Lord Jesus Christ quoted from Deuteronomy three times in His temptation in the wilderness. Surely a book so valuable to the Savior in such a time must also be valuable to us!

But where do you find Christ pictured in the book of Deuteronomy? Ada Habershon in *The Study of Types* lists 67 types and 13 contrasts between Moses and Christ. The Lord Jesus is seen in a twofold way in the book of Deuteronomy: by prophecy and by type.

These words of Moses are recorded in Deuteronomy 18:15, "The Lord thy God will raise up unto thee a Prophet from the midst of thee, of thy brethren, like unto me; unto Him ye shall hearken." After the Lord Jesus fed the 5,000 in Galilee, the people said, "This is of a truth that prophet that should come into the world" (John 6:14).

Shortly before the stones were hurled that crushed out the life of Stephen, that godly believer said about Jesus, "This is that Moses who said unto the children of Israel, A Prophet shall the Lord, your God, raise up unto you of your brethren, like me; Him shall ye hear" (Acts 7:37). Stephen indicated that Jesus Christ is the One of whom Moses spoke.

CHRIST PICTURED IN THE LIFE OF MOSES

The Scripture says that our Lord was a prophet "like unto Moses." Please consider the following points as you study Deuteronomy. Both Moses and Christ...

- were the object of a king's wrath.
- were goodly children.
- refused a kingdom (Hebrews 11:26).
- acted for the joy of the reward (Hebrews 12:2).
- were called out of Egypt.
- were made ruler over Israel.
- were rejected at first by their brethren.
- made the sea obey them.
- had people who wanted to stone them.
- delivered a parting blessing to Israel.
- had their resurrection contested (Jude 9; Matthew 17:3).
- were associated in the song of eternity (Revelation 15:3).

THE CITIES OF REFUGE

Six cities were appointed in Israel as cities of refuge: three on the east side of Jordan and three on the west (see Deuteronomy 4:41 and chapter 19). It may be that Hebrews 6:18 refers to this procedure. Highways led to the cities and the gates were always open. Jewish tradition says that signs with the word "refuge" on them were posted along the way. Runners were stationed along the highways into the cities. The cities of refuge were havens for those who committed murder unintentionally or through ignorance. Whenever that happened in Middle Eastern countries, an avenger would soon be on the track of that man.

What a wonderful picture of Christ's work! All mankind stands guilty. The avenger is on our trail, for "the wages of sin is death." We need a hiding place.

The cities of refuge were evenly placed throughout the land. Therefore, if a slayer fell into the hands of the avenger, it wasn't because a provision had not been made. But he had to make the choice to flee. Those cities were of Divine appointment, and the moment the slayer crossed the threshold he was safe. The avenger might brandish his sword at the gate, but he could not get in. The offender was tried by judges inside the city. Likewise, the believing sinner will not be tried by the world. We are judged in the courts of heaven.

The one who fled for refuge was allowed to stay until the death of the high priest. We have a High Priest who lives forever; therefore, we are eternally safe. The avenger can never lay his threatening sword upon us.

THE DEATH OF MOSES

The last chapter of Deuteronomy records the death of Moses. This man was a prince in Egypt for 40 years, a shepherd in the desert for 40 years, and the leader of Israel for 40 years. Did he make mistakes? Yes, but how faithfully he directed Israel! In his death (except that he was kept from entering the promised land because of his act of disobedience) we see striking similarities to the death and resurrection of our Lord.

1. Moses went up to die (v. 1). Christ ascended to Calvary.
2. He was alone, except for God (v. 6). Christ's followers forsook Him.
3. The Lord talked to him (v. 4).
4. His faculties were unimpaired (v. 7). Christ remained in control until His death.
5. What a funeral! He died "according to the word of the Lord" (v. 5); literally, "at the mouth of the Lord." Christ dismissed His own spirit when the work was completed.
6. This is not the last we see of Moses. He stood with Christ and Elijah on the mount of transfiguration 1500 years later. Evidently the devil tried to hold

the body of Moses so that he could not appear with the Lord Jesus (Jude 9). Death could not hold our Savior.

Satan may also wish to hold the bodies of believers in the ground, but his power is broken. The resurrected Christ has gained victory over him. Just as Satan could not prevent the appearance of Moses on the mount of transfiguration, so he cannot prevent the resurrection of those who have died in Christ. "When Christ, who is our life, shall appear, then shall ye also appear with Him in glory" (Colossians 3:4).

The concluding four chapters of Deuteronomy contain the farewell words of Moses. They celebrate the righteousness and grace of Jehovah in the history of Israel from the flood to the second coming of Christ. F. W. Grant in *The Numerical Bible* says, "But as a prophet in the nearness to God to which he [Moses] was called, he had no successor until He came who in His own Person stood alone, in life, in death, filling all the mediatorial types, and transcending them by the full measure of His infinite glory, in whose light indeed alone they shine."

JOSHUA

This book begins the second division of the Old Testament, which comprises 12 books and closes with Esther. The corresponding book to Joshua in the New Testament is the epistle to the Ephesians.

The word "Joshua" means "Jehovah is Savior," or "the Lord is salvation." The Greek name for Joshua is "Jesus." Therefore, we expect to find the book filled with typical teaching about Christ and His work in redemption. The Red Sea, for example, typifies what we are separated *from* and is fulfilled in Romans 6 and 7; the Jordan River typifies what we are separated *unto* and is fulfilled in Ephesians 1 and 2.

Joshua contains the record of about 25 years of Israel's history. We will consider some great truths about Christ and our relationship to Him that stand out in this book.

OUTLINE OF THE BOOK
    I. Jehovah's Command and Promise (1)
   II. Grace Abounding (2)
  III. Crossing the Jordan and Entering the
      Promised Land (3-5)
  IV. Conquest of the Land (6-12)

V. Distribution of the Land (13-21)
VI. Separation of the Peaceful Tribes (22)
VII. Joshua's Parting Address (23,24)

God's purpose for Israel was not only to deliver them out of Egypt but to bring them into the land of promise. Canaan does not represent heaven. Remember, Canaan had in it walled cities, giants, and chariots of iron. It was a land of conflict, but it was also a land of conquest. God has far more in store for us than simply saving us from the penalty of sin. He desires to give us victory in our present situation, and enables us to claim what is ours in Christ Jesus. "Blessed be the God and Father of our Lord Jesus Christ, who hath blessed us with all spiritual blessings in heavenly places in Christ" (Ephesians 1:3). "Jordan," according to Jerome, means "stream of judgment"; according to Augustine, "to come down." In either case it implies death to self, the experience through which every believer must pass to enter into the rest God intends for us.

The brevity of this book makes it necessary to limit our study to seven truths in Joshua that exemplify Christ and our relationship to Him.

JOSHUA

The book begins with the words, "Now after the death of Moses . . . " (1:1). Moses represented the law. The people could not enter the land of Canaan until Moses was dead. "For what the law could not do, in that it was weak through the flesh, God sending His own Son, in the likeness of sinful flesh and for sin, condemned sin in the flesh, that the righteousness of the law might be fulfilled in us, who walk not after the flesh, but after the Spirit" (Romans 8:3,4). Moses died; he could not lead the people in. Likewise, the flesh is weak. What Moses could not do, Joshua did. He led them through the Jordan, which speaks of death and resurrection. He led the children of Israel to victory after crossing the Jordan. He was their advocate in time of defeat. It was Joshua who allotted them their portions within the land. All of this beautifully pictures the work of our

Lord in death and resurrection, in His present advocacy at the Father's right hand, and in His provision for believers.

CHRIST

Not only is Christ typified in the life and ministry of Joshua, Israel's great warrior and deliverer, but we actually see Christ Himself in this marvelous book. Suppose someone should ask, "I thought Christ did not exist until Bethlehem. Where do you find Him in the book of Joshua?" Let's consider several factors.

Joshua and the Israelites stand before Jericho, a walled city. God has told them to capture it. Joshua goes on a survey trip around the city outside the walls. Suddenly he is confronted by a man with a drawn sword. Without question, this is a supernatural being. Joshua asks the question I think most of us would have asked: "Are you for us, or for our enemies?" A strange answer came from this supernatural being. "Nay, but as captain of the host of the Lord am I now come" (Joshua 5:14). In other words, this person was saying to Joshua, "I've not come to take your *part;* I've come to take your *place.*"

Joshua 6 indicates that this supernatural person was none other than the Lord Himself. What a lesson! Joshua was to learn of One who was adequate for the task and equal to the circumstance. Christian friend, let us not forget this in our work. None of us is sufficient for the assignment. But we have One "who is able to do exceedingly abundantly above all that we ask or think" (Ephesians 3:20). Yes, this was one of the pre-incarnate appearances of the Lord Jesus Christ.

THE FALL OF JERICHO

Jericho, a great walled city, presented a new possibility for Israel. Yet the Lord said to Joshua, "See, I have given into thine hand Jericho, and its king, and the mighty men of valor" (Joshua 6:2). Jehovah had a plan for the conquest of that city. Joshua and the children of Israel were to march around the city once a day for 6 days. They were to be preceded by the ark of the covenant and seven priests bearing seven trumpets of ram's horns. On the seventh day they were to compass the city seven times and the priests were to blow the trumpets. On that seventh day, and at the seventh blowing of a long blast of the ram's horn the people of Israel were to shout with a great shout. When they did, the walls of the city would fall down flat. The people were absolutely quiet until Joshua commanded them to shout. Then the walls collapsed and the city of Jericho was taken!

The great lesson for us is that spiritual victories are not won by human means. Hebrews 11 says, "By faith the walls of Jericho fell down" (v. 30). Faith in what? Faith in the unseen Captain of the Lord's hosts!

This great victory in the experience of Israel is a warning. The Lord is dishonored when His church is engaged in activity that stems from fleshly energy, rather than from faith and the empowering of the Holy Spirit.

RAHAB

Read the account in Joshua 2 of Rahab, the harlot who sheltered the spies of Israel. They promised her that she and her household would be spared when Israel took the city of Jericho if she would display a scarlet thread in the window. Her response to the offer was, "According unto your words, so be it" (Joshua 2:21).

The full gospel story is bound up in this incident. Consider how she pictures the sinner who comes to Christ.

1. She was unholy, and she lived in a condemned city.
2. She believed in the power of God.
3. She believed the promises of God's messengers.
4. She displayed the token and seal of her faith.
5. Her deliverance was complete.

In addition, Rahab became one of the line of Christ. How beautifully she stands as a reflection of us, sinners who also came into the family of Christ.

42

THE DEFEAT AT AI

Chapter 6 of Joshua records the marvelous victory at Jericho. Then follows chapter 7, which tells of Israel's crushing defeat at Ai. Hardly had the shouts of victory in Jericho died away than the mourning cries began over the tragedy at Ai. One man, Achan, and his household disobeyed God and took some of the spoils, but God held the entire nation responsible. The leaders of Israel had decided to send relatively few men against the little town of Ai, which showed that they were depending upon their own ability rather than God's. The men of Ai killed 36 Israelites and forced the others to flee. God's appraisal of the situation was this: "Israel has sinned" (Joshua 7:11).

Many lessons are to be learned from Israel's defeat at Ai. Power for the present circumstance does not come from past experience. Nor can we depend upon earnestness to take the place of holiness. All Israel, including Joshua, mourned the failure, but they should have been mourning over their sin. The most harmful kind of sin is secret sin. "He that covereth his sin shall not prosper" (Proverbs 28:13). Achan engaged in the sin of disobedience, followed by the sin of covetousness.

When the apostle Paul listed the terrible category of sins in 1 Corinthians 5, he said pointedly, "But now I have written unto you not to keep company, if any man that is called a brother be a fornicator, or covetous ... " (1 Corinthians 5:11). What disgrace is brought upon the cause of Christ and His church when believers are guilty of coveting and then try to cover it! When the sin of Achan was confessed and the nation cleansed, Ai fell easily into Israel's hands.

LEAGUE WITH THE GIBEONITES

Joshua 9 tells the story. News of the conquering Israelites swept through the land of Canaan. When the inhabitants of Gibeon heard that Joshua and the people of Israel had conquered Jericho and Ai, they sent some of their own number disguised in old garments and patched shoes, carrying old sacks and dry and moldy bread. They came to Joshua and posed as citizens of a far country. We read that the men of Israel "asked not counsel at the mouth of the Lord" (v. 14); rather, they acquiesced to the request of the deceivers when they said, "We are your servants; therefore, now, make ye a league with us" (v. 11). Joshua made peace with the Gibeonites and let them live, and the princes of the congregation of Israel sealed that pact with an oath. Thus Israel failed to destroy these inhabitants of the land, for the agreement forced her to let them live. Israel found herself tied up in covenant with these people, and it spelled trouble for years to come.

How often the church of Jesus Christ is stymied in her forward march and in the performance of the commands of Christ because of her consorting with the world! Compromise with worldly religion, worldly people, or worldly plans always hinders the church.

THE DEATH OF JOSHUA

Joshua was now an old man. He had led the children of Israel victoriously through the land of Canaan. At life's end, he called upon the people of Israel to continue serving the Lord (chapter 24). Here is part of his last message: "And if it seem evil unto you to serve the Lord, choose you this day whom ye will serve, whether the gods which your fathers served that were on the other side of the river, or the gods of the Amorites, in whose land ye dwell; but as for me and my house, we will serve the Lord" (v. 15). Joshua had determined early in his life to follow the Lord; now, at his decline, he again declares his intention. Our heavenly Joshua, the Lord Jesus Christ, walked His earthly pilgrimage in perfect obedience to the Father. Not once did He falter. He could say, lifting His face toward heaven, "I have finished the work which Thou gavest Me to do" (John 17:4). Unlike the earthly Joshua who died and remains buried, the Lord Jesus Christ arose from the dead and now lives at the right hand of God the Father. What a wonderful Savior is Jesus, our Lord!

JUDGES

Joshua had led the children of Israel into their own land. In his final message he appealed to them to "serve the Lord" (Joshua 24:15). The people's response is found in Joshua 24:24, "And the people said unto Joshua, The Lord our God will we serve, and His voice will we obey." Then followed a unique period in their history that covered about 330 years—the time of the judges.

OUTLINE OF THE BOOK

    I. Historical Introduction; Connection with
       Joshua (1:1-3:6)
    II. The History of the Judges (3:7-16:31)
    III. Spiritual and Moral Decline in Israel (17-21)

We will now consider six key factors in Judges.

ISRAEL'S POSITION

God had called Israel from among the nations to be a repository for His truth and the channel of His revelation. In addition, Israel was to be the avenue through whom the Redeemer would come. God had chosen Israel to be a pedestal on which He might display Himself to the nations of the world.

As Judges begins, we find Israel as a people in their own land. This nation had an elaborate tabernacle service. The glory-cloud stood over that structure. Great victories were being won by Israel's army. Surely God was with this people! Their God was not like the impotent gods of the nations around them. The searching question was this: would Israel keep her testimony pure and make God known again to the world?

ISRAEL'S GOVERNMENT

The form of government in Israel was a theocracy. This means that Jehovah was king of His people, administering His rule through the judges. A time would come in Israel's history when she would reject this form of government and ask for a human king. We are told in 1 Samuel 8:7, "And the Lord said unto Samuel, Hearken unto the voice of the people in all that they say unto thee; for they have not rejected thee, but they have rejected Me, that I should not reign over them."

ISRAEL'S FAILURE

The beginning of Israel's transgression, and her rejection of Jehovah as king, is seen in three recurring phrases in the book of Judges. In fact, this book presents one of the darkest pictures of the human condition in all the Bible. In Judges 3:7 we read, "And the children of Israel did evil in the sight of the Lord." Judges 2:14 says, "And [the Lord] sold them into the hands of their enemies." Next in order came the response recorded in Judges 3:15, "But when the children of Israel cried unto the Lord, the Lord raised them up a deliverer." These three statements represent sin, punishment, and deliverance—a cycle repeated over and over again during this era.

The book of Judges records seven awful apostasies, seven dreadful judgments, and seven divine deliverances. But after each cycle the spiritual tide of Israel had fallen a little lower.

THE REASON FOR FAILURE

God had given an explicit command to Israel concerning the inhabitants of the land of Canaan. Keep in mind that those inhabitants were steeped in heathen idolatry and that Israel was to be a separate people, worshiping only Jehovah. Deuteronomy 20:17 gives the command of Jehovah to Israel, "But thou shalt utterly destroy them . . . as the Lord thy God hath commanded thee." Under Joshua's leadership, Israel began to fulfill the commission. We read this phrase repeatedly in the book of Joshua: "utterly destroyed" (see Joshua 2:10; 6:21; 8:26; 10:1; 10:40; 11:21). But the spiritual atmosphere changed as indicated in Judges 1:28, "And it came to pass, when Israel was strong, that they put the Canaanites to forced labor, and did not utterly drive them out." This was disobedience to God's Word. Israel's association with the Canaanites did not raise the Canaanites to Israel's level; rather, Israel came down to their level. It is always the same — disobedience spells decline.

SPIRITUAL TEACHING

The book of Judges underscores these spiritual truths:

1. The consequence of sin is death. Sin that is not followed by confession and atonement always results in punishment.

2. The product of worldly associations is unrighteousness. The sin of idolatry was the greatest sin of Israel during the time of the judges. Probably in their desire to be rich, they made friends with the Canaanites. Soon they had adopted their idolatrous practices. The same thing happens today when Christians make their associations with the world in order to better their position.

3. The fruit of our unfaithfulness tests us. Judges 3:1 declares, "Now these are the nations which the Lord left, to test Israel by them, even as many of Israel as had not known all the wars of Canaan." The Israelites had been commanded to exterminate the utterly depraved inhabitants of Palestine, but they didn't obey the Lord. Now, God used these very nations to give His people so much trouble that they turned back to Him in repentance and faith. Romans 5:20 says, "But where sin abounded, grace did much more abound."

4. The Bible is our guide. Israel was to chart her course by the word of God, as we are to follow the written Word. Let us make sure that when we talk about Jesus we're talking about the Christ of the Bible. In his first epistle, John said, "And there are three that bear witness in earth, the Spirit, and the water, and the blood; and these three agree in one" (1 John 5:8). I have read in the *Book of the Friends* this statement, "Whatever any man says or does which is contrary to the Scriptures, though under the profession of the immediate guidance of the Holy Spirit, must be reckoned and accounted a mere delusion . . . . There can be no appeal from them to any other authority whatsoever."

Israel was dependent for guidance upon the word of Jehovah. We today also need in our voyage of life a chart—the Scriptures; a compass—the Holy Spirit; a Captain—the Lord Jesus Christ.

5. We have nothing in ourselves in which to glory. It was "not by might, nor by power, but by My Spirit, saith the Lord of hosts" (Zechariah 4:6). Periodically during those dark days of Israel's apostasy, God raised up special men and women to be judges in Israel. Not one of them would be considered by modern standards a person of unusual gift or stature. Let me list for you seven of these people used by God and give a brief statement concerning the background of each.

Othniel:	Caleb's youngest brother's son.
Ehud:	A left-handed man and an assassin.
Deborah:	A member of the physically weaker sex.
Gideon:	A member of an obscure family in the smallest tribe; he was threshing wheat by a secluded winepress when God called him.
Tola:	His name means "worm."
Jephthah:	An outcast, the son of a harlot.
Samson:	A Nazirite.

These people illustrate the principle stated in 1 Corinthians 1:27 and 28, "But God hath chosen the foolish things of the world to confound the wise; and God hath chosen the weak things of the world to confound the things which are mighty; and base things of the world, and things which are despised, hath God chosen, yea, and things which are not, to bring to nothing things that are." The reason for this is "that no flesh should glory in His presence" (v. 29).

OUR DELIVERER, THE LORD JESUS CHRIST

The men and women who filled the office of judge were used by the Lord as deliverers. Christ is our true deliverer. He is our Savior from sin, punishment, and defeat. "But thanks be to God, who giveth us the victory through our Lord Jesus Christ" (1 Corinthians 15:57).

The book of Judges closes with civil war, ruin, destruction, and these words: " . . . every man did that which was right in his own eyes" (Judges 21:25).

For further study, I suggest that you become familiar with the sequence of events in Judges. Study the book biographically, looking at the judges themselves. In many of them you will discover those characteristics that find complete fulfillment in the marvelous person and unparalleled work of the Lord Jesus Christ.

RUTH

The book of Ruth provides a postscript to the Judges. The story occurred during this time of strife and bloodshed. A famine swept through the land. Even Bethlehem, the most fertile of places, was affected. This beautiful narrative involving a family is a graphic picture of the gospel story—the redemption provided in Christ Jesus.

OUTLINE OF THE BOOK

Chapter 1: The family, having left the "house of bread," is *in a far country*. They long to return. Two words characterize chapter 1—yearning and returning.

Chapter 2: Ruth is *in a field*, seeking and serving.

Chapter 3: Ruth is *at the door*. She has been received.

Chapter 4: What better place could Ruth be than *within the house*, chosen and rewarded?

THE NAMES IN RUTH

Old Testament names often have great significance. The Hebrew language puts much importance upon names, both those of men and those of God. Following are the principal characters of Ruth and the meanings of their names. For further study, associate the meanings with the story and note the typology.

Elimelech .... "My God is King"
Bethlehem...................... "House of Bread"
Moab......................... "Under the Curse"
Naomi................................ "Present"
Mahlon................................... "Sick"
Chilion .... "Pining"
Orpah .... "Fawn"
Ruth .... "Friendship," or "Beauty"
Mara .... "Bitter"
Boaz .... "Strength"

Let us now turn to a study of the typical teaching of this tender Old Testament story.

I. RUTH: A PORTRAYAL OF THE BELIEVING SINNER

Ruth was a Moabitess, not an Israelite. God had commanded, "[A] Moabite shall not enter into the congregation of the Lord" (Deuteronomy 23:3). Moabites were cut off from the covenant relationship Israel had with God. This is also the position of Gentiles by nature, and it describes us before we were saved by grace. Paul wrote, "That at that time ye were without Christ, being aliens from the commonwealth of Israel, and strangers from the covenants of promise, having no hope, and without God in the world" (Ephesians 2:12). Moab was under the curse of God.

II. RUTH: A PICTURE OF CHRISTIAN EXPERIENCE

Review the brief chapter outline with the following scriptural corroboration in mind:

Ruth Deciding (chapter 1). Poignant words of Ruth to Naomi appear in verse 16, "Entreat me not to leave thee, or to turn away from following after thee; for where thou goest, I will go; and where thou lodgest, I will lodge: thy people shall be my people, and thy God, my God." This is like the believing sinner's experience as stated in Romans 10:9,10, "That if thou shalt confess with thy mouth the Lord Jesus, and shalt believe in thine heart that God hath raised Him from the dead, thou shalt be saved. For with the heart man believeth unto righteousness; and with the mouth confession is made unto salvation."

Ruth Serving (chapter 2). Ruth went out into the field to glean ears of grain. Having made her decision to go with the people of God to Bethlehem, the "house of bread," she now takes the place of service. Romans 6:22 says, "But now being made free from sin, and become servants to God, ye have your fruit unto holiness, and the end everlasting life." The apostle Paul declared to the believers at Corinth, "For we preach not ourselves, but Christ Jesus the Lord, and ourselves your servants for Jesus' sake" (2 Corinthians 4:5).

Ruth Resting (chapter 3). What a beautiful scene! Ruth lay at the feet of Boaz, as was the Eastern custom. She was assured that he would do for her all that she needed. We read in Hebrews 4:10, "For he that is entered into his rest, he also hath ceased from his own works, as God did from His."

Ruth Rewarded (chapter 4). What an amazing story of grace! Boaz took Ruth unto himself as his wife, but when he did, all the inheritance he had purchased became hers. From that precious union came children and much blessing. The New Testament picture? "Blessed be the God and Father of our Lord Jesus Christ, who hath blessed us with all spiritual blessings in heavenly places in Christ, according as He hath chosen us in Him before the foundation of the world, that we should be holy and without blame before Him, in love" (Ephesians 1:3,4).

III. RUTH: A PORTRAIT OF THE FULLNESS OF REDEMPTION

Three great words may be placed over this brief Old Testament story: Pardoned! Purchased! Placed! Naomi's words to Ruth are striking. "Sit still, my daughter, until thou know how the matter will fall; for the man will not be in rest, until he have finished the thing this day" (Ruth 3:18).

Every Christian has this assurance from God's Word: "Being confident of this very thing, that He who hath begun a good work in you will perform it until the day of Jesus Christ" (Philippians 1:6). Ruth already had some measures of barley that were proof and pledge of the fullness that was to come.

IV. NAOMI: AN EXAMPLE OF COMFORT FOR BACKSLIDDEN SAINTS

The author of Hebrews said, "Whom the Lord loveth He chasteneth." Naomi, who with her family had gone into the far country away from the "house of bread," comes home, driven by loneliness and hunger. "She had heard in the country of Moab how the Lord had visited His people in giving them food" (1:6). We are told that "they came to Bethlehem in the beginning of barley harvest" (v. 22). In the far country she had lost her husband in death. Her two sons became ill and died. How often God allows heartache, tragedy, and trouble to beset the path of His children who have strayed! He uses chastisement to bring them back to Himself.

V. BOAZ: PICTURE OF CHRIST, OUR KINSMAN-REDEEMER

It helps to become thoroughly familiar with the principles that were applied when Boaz redeemed the land that had belonged to Elimelech and restored it to Naomi and Ruth. I suggest that you read carefully the law of the kinsman-redeemer as stated in Leviticus 25. The following observations are significant:

1. *Kinsman-redemption involved both person and inheritance.* The levitical law stated, "After he is sold he may be redeemed again; one of his brethren may redeem him" (Leviticus 25:48). We read tremendous news in Galatians 4:4,5, "But, when the fullness of the time was come, God sent forth His Son, made of a woman, made under the law, to redeem them that were under the law, that we might receive the adoption of sons." Boaz redeemed the parcel of land so that he might restore it to Naomi. He also removed all of the en-

cumbrances that were necessarily upon her and Ruth.

2. *The redeemer had to be a relative.* "Any that is near of kin unto him of his family may redeem him" (Leviticus 25:49). The Lord Jesus took our nature upon Himself to redeem us. Although He is called "the last Adam" (1 Corinthians 15:4,5), He was not tainted by Adam's transgression in any way. He had no sin in Himself, for He was "holy, harmless, undefiled, separate from sinners" (Hebrews 7:26). Yet He "made Himself of no reputation, and took upon Him the form of a servant, and was made *in the likeness of men*" (Philippians 2:7).

3. *The redeemer had to be able to redeem.* The law not only required the redemption of the property but also included the obligation to raise up seed to the deceased. As the kinsman-redeemer, Boaz was not only to buy back the property but he was also to take Ruth as his wife so that she might bear children. In Ruth's case, the first one in line to do this was unable to fulfill the obligation. Likewise, the law, the "first in line," was weak through the flesh and unable to redeem. But there is One! "Their Redeemer is strong, the Lord of hosts is His name" (Jeremiah 50:34). Here is what our great Kinsman-Redeemer said in John 10:11, "I am the good shepherd; the good shepherd giveth His life for the sheep." Look also at verse 18, "No man taketh it from Me, but I lay it down of Myself. I have power to lay it down, and I have power to take it again." Our Redeemer is able to redeem!

4. *The kinsman-redeemer had to pay the price in full.* The levitical law demanded, "Then let him count the years of the sale thereof, and restore the overpayment unto the man to whom he sold it" (Leviticus 25:27). This meant that the full price and more was to be paid for the land. Nothing was to be lacking; the payment was to be in full. "Forasmuch as ye know that ye were not redeemed with corruptible things, like silver and gold, from your vain manner of life received by tradition from your fathers, but with the precious blood of Christ, as of a lamb without blemish and without spot"

(1 Peter 1:18,19). With the poet we rejoice, "Free from the law, O happy condition;/ Jesus has died and there is remission./ Cursed by the law and bruised by the fall,/ Christ has redeemed us, once for all!"

We can only skim the surface. Christ is seen prominently in the book of Ruth as the Kinsman-Redeemer. In the words of one biblical commentator, "Add a Ruth postscript to the living epistle of your life; make Jesus your Lord, and rest in Him."

1 SAMUEL

The book of 1 Samuel is a book of transition. It outlines the change from the theocracy established under Moses to the monarchy begun under Saul. The book also marks the transition from priests to prophets as the central figure of God's dealing with Israel. First Samuel is really a continuation of the book of Judges, with Ruth as a parenthesis. The key thought is "choosing a king," and the key verse reads, "Now, therefore, behold the king whom ye have chosen" (1 Samuel 12:13).

OUTLINE OF THE BOOK

I. Close of the Period of the Judges (1-7)
- A. Early life of Samuel (1-3)
- B. Judgments on Eli and loss of the ark (4:1-7:2)
- C. Samuel as judge (7:3-17)

II. Beginning of the Monarchy (8-31)
- A. Appointment of the first king (8-10)
- B. Saul's reign until his rejection (11-15)
- C. The fall of Saul and rise of David (16-31)

As the book of 1 Samuel opens, lawlessness is reaching its height in Israel. The threshold of the book also depicts in symbol the spiritual state of Israel. After first considering the significance of losing the ark of the covenant, we shall see how Samuel and David reflect Christ, and how Saul represents his countertype.

THE LOSS OF THE ARK

Chapter 4 of 1 Samuel records the story. The people had forgotten God. The priesthood was corrupted. Eli, the high priest, had no control over his sons, who were also priests. We are told, "Wherefore the sin of the young men was very great before the Lord; for men abhorred the offering of the Lord" (1 Samuel 2:17). How sad! Men who had no real knowledge of God were in charge of holy things.

To make matters worse, the Philistine armies had moved up against Israel and were defeating them. So the elders of Israel decided to get the ark of the covenant from Shiloh and carry it into battle. They reasoned this way: "It may save us out of the hand of our enemies" (1 Samuel 4:3). The ark symbolized God's presence with His people. But Israel failed to distinguish between having a form of godliness and knowing God's presence in their midst. Not only was Israel defeated in the battle with the Philistines, but that heathen people also killed the two sons of Eli and captured the ark. Ungodly men cannot preserve the power of true faith. They turn the most holy things into ridicule. Furthermore, the Lord will not protect empty ritual when the Spirit is gone. Sin always brings defeat.

But let's get back to the primary thought of these studies. Perhaps someone is asking, "Where in this book of apostasy, sin, and defeat do we see the Lord Jesus?" First Samuel is really a biography of three men: Samuel, Saul, and David. We shall consider each of them, probing to see how the Lord Jesus is pictured either by comparison or contrast.

SAMUEL

The Lord Jesus is pictured often in the life of Samuel. During that period when Eli and his licentious sons occupied the office of the priesthood, a glimmer of hope came to the land in the person of a praying mother. Take note of the fact that conditions in Israel just prior to our Lord's first coming were similar. To Hannah was born a son whom she called "Samuel." That name means "heard of God" or "sons of God." Read again Hannah's prayer in the first ten verses of 1 Samuel 2. This prayer was prophetic, looking forward to a day of deliverance. An interesting parallel can be observed in the prayer of Hannah and Mary's prayer, the Magnificat, recorded in Luke 1:46-55.

Similarities between Christ and Samuel may be seen in the growth of Samuel, his acceptance as prophet and priest, and his place as ruler. Samuel's activity was terminated when the people, demanding a king, rejected him (1 Samuel 8:7).

SAUL

The people did not want Samuel as their judge and ruler; consequently, God let them have a king of their choosing. By comparison, how pertinent are these words of our Lord: "I am come in My Father's name, and ye receive Me not; if another shall come in his own name, him ye will receive" (John 5:43).

So Saul was chosen king over Israel. He was head and shoulders above other men. He made an awesome sight as he stood among the people. The "morning" of Saul's life was calm and bright. How wonderful if he would have said something like, "Take my life and let it be consecrated, Lord, to Thee"! But no. "There is a line by us unseen/ But crosses every path,/ The hidden boundary between/ God's patience and His wrath." Saul had crossed that line. Consequently, the "midday" of his life was cloudy and threatening. His "afternoon" was cold and dark; his "evening" was terrifying with the thunderstorms of despair and suicidal blackness.

Much about Saul suggests Satan's counterfeit, Antichrist. The Lord Jesus came in the Father's name and was rejected. Antichrist will come like Saul of old, the people's choice. He will be received and exalted. But he will bring a holocaust of war, famine, despair, and death.

DAVID

A child was born in Bethlehem of the tribe of Judah. This lad, who was destined to be Israel's greatest king, spent his youth in his father's fields. How like our Lord, who spent His childhood in Joseph's carpenter's shop.

David was anointed as king long before he was recognized. He was sought and hunted by Saul, who desired his death even though he had done nothing to deserve it. David's first public act was the meeting of Goliath; similarly, our Lord's first experience following His baptism was His temptation by Satan in the wilderness.

The first part of David's reign was met with great acclaim by the nation. The Lord Jesus was met in His triumphal entry with cries of "Hosanna to the son of David!"

It was not long, though, until David was rejected by Israel and had to hide in the cave of Adullam. John tells us that Jesus "came unto His own, and His own received Him not" (John 1:11). A strange company of men gathered with David in that cave—some 400 of them. Who were they? They were the distressed, the debtors, the discontented. But somehow they were attracted to David. The inspired writer to the Hebrews said, "Let us go forth, therefore, unto Him outside the camp, bearing His reproach" (Hebrews 13:13). You would find it most interesting to read the story of these men who joined David and who were faithful to him at the time of his rejection (2 Samuel 23:8-39). Paul wrote to young Timothy, "If we suffer, we shall also reign with Him; if we deny Him, He also will deny us" (2 Timothy 2:12).

Christ is the anointed of God. No doubt about it, Jesus Christ will reign! However, we are living in the time of His rejection. It will not always be so, for coronation time is coming!

2 SAMUEL

This book tells the story of one person, David. It could appropriately be called "the acts of King David." One thousand years after David, the Lord Jesus Christ was born of his seed and lineage. He was David's son and David's Lord. Consequently, we can expect 2 Samuel to be full of teaching concerning Christ.

The time covered by the book is limited to about 38 years of Israel's history. It tells of David's early training as a shepherd, as a servant to the king, and as a warrior in hiding. This sets a fitting backdrop for David's later life, where he is seen in three aspects:

- A wonderful shepherd to his people
- A wise king as he rules
- A tough soldier who fights courageously

As Saul is pictured in 1 Samuel as the people's choice, so 2 Samuel pictures David as God's choice.

OUTLINE OF THE BOOK

I. David's Eulogy for Saul and Jonathan (1)
II. David's Reign at Hebron (2-4)
III. David's Reign over all Israel at Jerusalem (5-10)

IV. David's Great Sin and Its Punishment (11-21)
V. David's Song of Deliverance and Last
Words (22,23)
VI. David's Numbering of Israel (24)

Limiting our consideration of 2 Samuel to a single brief chapter is most difficult. So that we may condense some of the great truths found in this book, we will think of it historically, prophetically, and typically.

HISTORICAL TEACHING

Chapter 5 of 2 Samuel reports that David moved up against Jerusalem, captured it, and made it the capital of his kingdom. We learn later that this city also became the center of the worship of Jehovah. This is actually the third time Jerusalem is mentioned in the Bible. The first occurs in Genesis 14, where Abraham, returning from the rescue of Lot, was met by Melchizedek, priest-king of Salem, and gave a tithe to God. (Psalm 76, a psalm of Asaph, also refers to Jerusalem with the term "Salem.")

The second mention of the city is found in Judges 1:8, which records how Judah drove the Jebusites from the city and burned it, even though the Jebusites remained in control of the citadel.

The third, here in chapter 5 of 2 Samuel, tells how it became the capital of the Davidic kingdom. The history of Jerusalem, the most important spot on the face of the globe, begins here. Another writer has said, "If Palestine is the theater of the world's dreams, then Jerusalem is the stage." The psalmist wrote of Jerusalem, "Beautiful for situation, the joy of the whole earth, is Mount Zion, on the sides of the north, the city of the great King" (Psalm 48:2). From the days of David until this present time, Jerusalem has been the center of the world's attention. In some ways, it has been the "storm center."

You will find it most helpful to trace the history of Jerusalem, beginning with 1055 B.C. and proceeding until New Testament days. Much of this history can be learned by reading the following passages of Scripture:

1 Kings 14:25,26; 2 Chronicles 12:2; 2 Kings 14:13; 2 Chronicles 25; 2 Kings 16:5; 2 Chronicles 28; Daniel 1:1; Ezekiel 1:1; 2 Kings 25:1; Jeremiah 32:28-30; Ezra 3:1-3; 2:1-70; 4:4-24; 7:21.

The greatest event in the history of the world, the crucifixion and resurrection of the Lord Jesus Christ, took place at Jerusalem.

If you thumb the pages of the history of Jerusalem after our Lord's birth, you will find that the sands of Israel, and especially the environs of that city, have been drenched with the blood of rampaging armies. The city has been beseiged approximately 20 times since A.D. 70. Why? Not because of its maritime value, for it is not on the sea. Not because of its population, for other cities have exceeded it by millions. But somehow it is a strategic center. It has a purpose in the economy of God, and Satan wants to control it.

As we examine carefully the prophetic Word, we find that many great events are yet destined to take place there. God will one day gather all the nations against Jerusalem to battle. Jehovah Himself will fight against them (Zechariah 14:2,3). The Lord Jesus Christ will return to the Mount of Olives, which is located just east of Jerusalem (Zechariah 14:4). Jerusalem will become the capital of the millennial kingdom (Zechariah 8:20-23). And the law and the word of the Lord will go forth from that city (Isaiah 2:1-3).

Jerusalem has repeatedly been caught between opposing armies; it has often been "the iron between the triphammer and the anvil." But a day is coming when Jerusalem will become a "quiet habitation, a tabernacle that shall not be taken down" (Isaiah 33:20).

PROPHETIC TEACHING

A main prophetic teaching of 2 Samuel is found in the Davidic covenant, spelled out in chapter 7, verses 14 through 16. This is one of the mountainpeaks of Scripture! The covenant with David was confirmed by God's own oath, for Jehovah said, "I have made a covenant with My chosen, I have sworn unto David, My servant:

Thy seed will I establish forever, and build up thy throne to all generations" (Psalm 89:3,4). God further stated, "Once have I sworn by My holiness that I will not lie unto David. His seed shall endure forever, and his throne as the sun before Me" (Psalm 89:35,36).

Note the five terms of the Davidic covenant:
1. a Davidic house—a posterity
2. a throne—a royal authority
3. a kingdom—a sphere of rule
4. a perpetuity—forever
5. a promise—disobedience followed by chastisement, but no abrogation

These promises are carried over into the New Testament. Acts 15:14 gives us the divine program for the church age, and the Davidic covenant will be fulfilled when this age is completed.

TYPICAL TEACHING

As much as any book in the Old Testament, 2 Samuel demonstrates the grace of God. David himself received God's grace time and time again. This is shown markedly in his awful sin, his restoration, and his assurance of God's forgiveness.

David's care of Mephibosheth is a picture of the sinner received, forgiven, and exalted to a place of fellowship and provision. Consider these reflections of God's redeeming grace in Christ:
1. Mephibosheth was lame (2 Samuel 4:4), having fallen at the hands of another.
2. He was sought by David even though he belonged to the family of the king's enemies (9:1-3).
3. He was found in the house of Machir (9:5). "Machir" means "sold."
4. He was in the land of Lodebar which means "no pasture" (9:5).
5. He feared the king (9:6).
6. He took the place of humility before David (9:6). This reminds us of the publican and the prodigal.

7. David gave him the highest place (9:10). How full is God's measure of grace!

8. He lived in the city of Jerusalem, which means "peace" (9:13).

9. He carried the marks of his fall to his grave, but grace kept them out of sight (9:13).

All of this speaks volumes about the work of our Lord in making possible the salvation of sinners and about our acceptance before Him. A tremendous Messianic note is sounded in 2 Samuel 19:10, "Now, therefore, why speak ye not a word of bringing the king back?" The Davidic covenant will find its fulfillment in David's greater Son, the Lord Jesus Christ, who will one day return.

1 KINGS

The books of Samuel, Kings, and Chronicles present the history of the Kingdom of Israel. The first four give it from a human standpoint, and in Chronicles, it is seen from God's viewpoint.

The time covered by 1 Kings is about 120 years. The book begins with the death of David and closes with the death of Ahab. One Bible scholar has said, "During this time the nation passes from affluence and influence to poverty and paralysis." The tragic note sounded in 1 Kings 11:1 marks a turning point in Israel's history. "But King Solomon loved many foreign women...." As a result, the flesh prevailed over the Spirit. We therefore read these sad words in 1 Kings 11:4, "When Solomon was old, ... his wives turned away his heart after other gods."

When 1 Kings opens, Samuel is dead and David is dying. Chapter 2 tells how this shepherd, warrior, king, and psalmist went to be with the Lord. Solomon, David's son, then ascended to the throne of all Israel. This book is important because it tells a story of sharp contrast: first, Israel's greatest splendor; second, Israel's tragic downfall. After Solomon's death there was a rebellion. The nation divided into two kingdoms—Israel in the north and Judah in the south. King after king led the people into idolatry. It's the old story of sin followed by punishment.

Two men stand out more conspicuously than all the rest named in 1 Kings—Solomon and Elijah. The story really centers upon these two leaders. As we study these men, we fulfill the purpose for this volume—to see Christ in every book of the Old Testament.

SOLOMON'S REIGN

The name Solomon means "peace." His reign is a type or picture of that reign of peace by Him who is greater than Solomon. Solomon's reign was notable for five outstanding reasons:

1. *Wisdom* (1 Kings 3:9-12; 4:29-34). Jewish legend says that Solomon could even converse with the beasts of the field. His proverbs, 3,000 of which are recorded, demonstrate the great wisdom that God had given him. What marvelous guidelines they are for the conduct of life even now!

2. *Peace and prosperity* (4:25). Solomon's reign was an unusual time for Israel. The land had been torn apart by war. Now came a time of calm, of peace. "And Judah and Israel dwelt safely, every man under his vine and under his fig tree, from Dan even unto Beersheba, all the days of Solomon" (1 Kings 4:25).

3. *The building of the temple* (chapters 5-7). Solomon's temple was unsurpassed in his day for its splendor and luxury. It was the crown jewel of Solomon's reign. Out of Israel came 30,000 men working in relays of 10,000 per month. In addition, 150,000 "strangers," 70,000 of them carriers and 80,000 stone workers, along with 3,300 supervisors, assisted in the work.

4. *God enters the temple* (chapter 8). When the structure was completed and dedicated, the glory cloud, the shekinah, came down and filled it. This was the visible manifestation of the presence of God in the midst of His people.

5. *The visit of the Queen of Sheba* (chapter 10). This

influential ruler said to Solomon, "It was a true report that I heard in mine own land of thy acts and of thy wisdom" (10:6). The wealthy ruler was so impressed with what she had heard and seen that she gave the glory to God, saying, "Blessed be the Lord thy God, who delighted in thee, to set thee on the throne of Israel" (v. 9). A Gentile queen beholding the wealth and beauty of Solomon's reign is a picture of what God has yet in store for this earth.

ONE GREATER THAN SOLOMON

The gospel according to Matthew begins with the words, "The book of the genealogy of Jesus Christ, the son of David." The designation "son of David" immediately brings Solomon to mind, arrayed in all his kingly glory. His reign is a foreview of what will take place when David's greater Son, the Lord Jesus Christ, rules over the earth.

God has decreed that a man is going to rule this world in wisdom. Isaiah wrote, "And there shall come forth a rod out of the stem of Jesse, and a Branch shall grow out of his roots; and the Spirit of the Lord shall rest upon Him, the spirit of wisdom and understanding, the spirit of counsel and might, the spirit of knowledge and of the fear of the Lord, ... but with righteousness shall He judge the poor, and reprove with equity for the meek of the earth; and He shall smite the earth with the rod of His mouth, and with the breath of His lips shall He slay the wicked" (Isaiah 11:1,2,4).

Our Lord's millennial reign will be a time of peace and prosperity. The prophet Micah declared of Christ, "And He shall judge among many people, and rebuke strong nations afar off; and they shall beat their swords into plowshares, and their spears into pruning hooks; nation shall not lift up a sword against nation, neither shall they learn war anymore. But they shall sit every man under his vine and under his fig tree, and none shall make them afraid; for the mouth of the Lord of hosts hath spoken it" (Micah 4:3,4).

A temple will again stand in old Jerusalem. If you

study carefully Ezekiel 40 through 49, you will learn about this magnificent edifice. The glory of the Lord will fill that place, and people of all nations will come to it. Micah predicted,

Many nations shall come, and say, Come, and let us go up to the mountain of the Lord, and to the house of the God of Jacob (Micah 4:2).

Zechariah delivered this additional prophecy:

And it shall be, in that day, that living waters shall go out from Jerusalem; half of them toward the former sea, and half of them toward the hinder sea; in summer and in winter shall it be.

And the Lord shall be king over all the earth; in that day shall there be one Lord, and His name one.

And it shall come to pass that everyone that is left of all the nations which came against Jerusalem shall even go up from year to year to worship the King, the Lord of hosts, and to keep the feast of tabernacles (Zechariah 14:8,9,16).

FROM KINGS TO PROPHETS

How tragic the change! Chapter 10 tells of Solomon and all his glory. Then chapter 11 tells of Solomon's sin, chronicles the beginning of the rebellion by Jeroboam, and records Solomon's death. The division of the kingdom and fall into idolatry soon followed. We naturally wonder why. The answer, of course, is that fallen man spoils everything he touches.

From this point onward, the Lord God no longer revealed Himself primarily to kings; rather, He turned to the prophets. From 1 Kings 11 to the beginning of the New Testament, God spoke to His people primarily through these specially chosen men.

ELIJAH

The experiences of Elijah the prophet give us a challenge for today, for he was active in a time of apostasy. The end of our age will also be marked by apostasy, so a study of the evil men of Elijah's day will tell us what may be expected. The same conditions exist now as did then. Ahab had married Jezebel. This wicked woman introduced Baal worship and other forms of idolatry. Ahab was sitting in the place of authority on the throne of Israel, yet he was denying the God of Israel. Similar conditions are sometimes seen in the conduct of the religious leaders of our day.

In 1 Kings 18 we read of two prophets, Obadiah and Elijah. Obadiah feared the Lord and fed the prophets of God who were hiding in a cave. But he lived in the house of Ahab, a compromising position! Ahab never spoke a word against Obadiah. But concerning Elijah, the wicked king said, "Art thou he who troubleth Israel?" (18:17). Elijah did not shrink from a confrontation with Ahab. God's exoneration of Elijah took place on Mount Carmel, and that prophet became the instrument of God's judgment upon the prophets of both Baal and the groves.

PRACTICAL TRUTH

In 1 Kings, one truth looms large on the horizon: a government that leaves God out, whether dictatorship or democracy, is doomed to failure. Government by man always ends in disorder. Yet even though the thrones of earth disintegrate, the throne in heaven will abide forever.

2 KINGS

We now come to perhaps the saddest book of all Jewish history. It records the carrying away into captivity of Israel by Assyria in 721 B.C. and the captivity of Judah by Babylon in 586 B.C. Second Kings is often called the "book of dispersion." In 1 Kings we read that Solomon succeeded David, and we saw how Israel reached the zenith of her earthly splendor. But Solomon failed. He sinned by unduly taxing the people to support his lifestyle, and the kingdom was divided.

The result of his sin was God's hand of chastening. This is expressed best in what many consider to be the key verse of 2 Kings, "In those days the Lord began to cut off a part of Israel" (10:32).

The reader will better understand the setting and circumstances in Israel and Judah if he will read the prophetic books written during that time. To Israel: Amos and Hosea. To Judah: Obadiah, Joel, Isaiah, Micah, Nahum, Habakkuk, Zephaniah, and Jeremiah.

OUTLINE OF THE BOOK

I. Israel and Judah until the Fall of Samaria (1-17)

II. The History of Judah to the Destruction of Jerusalem (18-25)

The book of 2 Kings opens with the record of Elijah's translation, the succession of Elisha, and the wonderful shout, "The spirit of Elijah doth rest on Elisha" (2:15). The book closes with the sad plight of King Jehoiachin (25:27-30). The book begins with the blessing from heaven upon God's prophet; it closes with the king of Judah under a regular allowance from a heathen ruler (v. 30).

Second Kings is filled with teaching concerning Christ, even though His name is not mentioned. The ministry of Elisha, whose name means "my God is salvation," is a graphic picture of our Lord Jesus Christ in the midst of abounding evils. Let us consider three of these pictures.

CHRIST AND THE BELIEVER (2:1-22)

As you consider the account of the translation of Elijah into heaven and the transfer of his power to Elisha, you almost feel as if you are reading the first chapters of the book of Acts.

Elijah ascended into heaven bodily, personally, and visibly. Note the progression of Elisha's walk to power. He refused to remain at Gilgal, the place where the reproach of Egypt had been rolled away. He went with Elijah to Bethel, "the house of God." But he needed more than that. So he proceeded with the prophet from Bethel to Jericho, the place of the curse. But a further step followed in the progression. He walked on to the Jordan, the place of death, and passed through the river with Elijah and on to the other side. This says to the believer that we reckon ourselves "to be dead indeed unto sin, but alive unto God through Jesus Christ, our Lord" (Romans 6:11).

Then, like Christ's disciples centuries later, Elisha watched his mentor being taken up from him into heaven (2:11). Take note of the energy of his faith! True faith always counts upon God's faithfulness. Elisha had met God's conditions, so he expected God to fulfill His part. By faith he took the mantle of Elijah and struck the waters, and they parted. Then he came back across the Jordan the same way he had gone. The power of Elijah was his.

All of this is a beautiful picture of our identification with the Lord Jesus in His death, His resurrection, His ascension, and His present position at the Father's right hand. And, as the spirit of Elijah became Elisha's, so the Holy Spirit indwells the believer to demonstrate through him the resurrection life of the Lord Jesus Christ.

CHRIST AND THE WORD (4:38-41)

The land was plagued with a drought. Every effort had failed; famine had spread throughout the nation. Even a superficial consideration of this account brings to mind similarities to the present spiritual condition in Christendom.

Not only was there dearth in the land, there was also "death in the pot." The food had been poisoned with wild gourds. Those who were to partake of the food did not know of this deadly ingredient. In the New Testament, our Lord warned of "leaven" that had been slipped into the flour. And Jude says that "certain men crept in unawares, . . . ungodly men, turning the grace of our God into lasciviousness, and denying the only Lord God, and our Lord Jesus Christ" (Jude 4). God's children are to be alert to any "death in the pot," any infiltration of sin and error.

How are we to counteract evil's presence? In the biblical account, Elisha ordered meal to be brought and cast into the pot. In the feasts of Jehovah and the sacrifices of the tabernacle, meal pictured the Word of God. That is the antidote for theological poison! "To the law and to the testimony; if they speak not according to this word, it is because there is no light in them" (Isaiah 8:20). The Lord Jesus prayed, "Sanctify them through Thy truth; Thy word is truth" (John 17:17). Although the written Word of God reveals the living Word, the Lord Jesus, they are inseparable. False doctrine can be counteracted only by the preaching and the teaching of the Bible.

CHRIST AND THE SINNER (5:1-14)

The cleansing of Naaman the leper is a gem among Old Testament stories. This incident depicts beautifully the provision God has made in Christ for one afflicted with the terrible leprosy of sin.

Although Naaman had an exalted position with the king of Syria, was honored by his master, and was a courageous man, the fatal word concerning him is stated starkly in the account. "He was a leper." Leprosy speaks of the defilement of sin, which afflicts every individual. Regardless of fine heredity, acquired culture, extensive education, or moral character, man in the sight of God is a spiritual leper. "There is none righteous, no, not one" (Romans 3:10).

This thrilling story of a great man's cleansing is highlighted by the faithful witness of a little maid who had been taken captive into Syria. She was a servant in Naaman's household, and she bore fruitful testimony to God's power through His servant Elisha. The Holy Spirit chooses to use men and women, boys and girls, to give the message of redeeming grace in Christ. Our Lord said to His disciples, "But ye shall receive power, after the Holy Spirit is come upon you; and ye shall be witnesses unto Me" (Acts 1:8).

Satan bitterly opposes the operation of the Word of God and the Spirit of God in the work of cleansing spiritual lepers. This is seen clearly in the account of Naaman, where three forces worked against his recovery from leprosy. We read first that he went to the king of Israel rather than the prophet Elisha (2 Kings 5:5).

Second, Naaman had a preconceived idea of the way his cleansing should be accomplished. How like human nature to want some show of the flesh, some spectacular demonstration, rather than simply believing the Word! Naaman said, "I thought, he will surely come out to me, and stand, and call on the name of the Lord his God, and strike his hand over the place, and cure the leprosy" (v. 11).

The third form of opposition came in the form of prejudice. The leper said, "We have better rivers than this at home" (see v. 12). This tendency is often seen today in the stringent denominational formulas that add to the pure gospel. They mix in such demands as joining their church or submitting to some ordinance in order to be assured of salvation. Cleansing for Naaman came only when he obeyed the word of God's prophet and went into the only river specified. No "rivers" of man's choosing can ever remove the guilt of sin. There is only one way. "The blood of Jesus Christ, His Son, cleanseth us from all sin" (1 John 1:7).

1 CHRONICLES

The books of Chronicles repeat much of the history recorded in Kings. The events of 1 Chronicles parallel those of 2 Samuel, but they are seen through the eyes of the priest rather than the prophet. The book concentrates upon the history of Judah, speaking of Israel only when it comes in contact with the people and events of the Southern Kingdom.

Chronicles has been called by some "the chosen book of the theocracy." It tells the story of a great king and points forward to an even greater King and kingdom. First Chronicles 17:24 sets the theme, "Let the house of David, Thy servant, be established before Thee."

OUTLINE OF THE BOOK

    I. The Royal Genealogy (1-9)
    II. The Parenthesis of Saul's Rule (10)
    III. The Reign of David (11-29)

We will discuss three of the key questions that arise when one studies 1 Chronicles.

THE REASON FOR THE GENEALOGIES

We read in 2 Timothy 3:16 and 17 that "All Scripture is given by inspiration of God, and is profitable for doctrine, for reproof, for correction, for instruction in righteousness, that the man of God may be perfect, thoroughly furnished unto all good works." The genealogies of 1 Chronicles 1-9 fall within the scope of this passage. They are profitable for at least three reasons. First, they were of great benefit to the Jews who returned from captivity in Babylon. During this time of confusion the Israelites were in danger of losing their family and tribal identities. The lists helped them maintain their distinctives. Second, the genealogies impressed the Jews with the unity of God. As they returned from captivity, the Israelites saw in the genealogies that the God who had restored them was the "one true God" of their fathers. Third, the genealogies were a demonstration of the divine purpose being worked out until Christ's coming. They helped complete the Bible story of our Savior, who was the son of David, the son of Judah, the son of Abraham, and the son of Adam. He took their humanity, "yet without sin."

THE ARK BROUGHT TO JERUSALEM

As 1 Chronicles opens, David has been anointed king over Israel, and he is making preparation to bring the ark back to Jerusalem. The events that preceded this are recorded in 1 Samuel 4-6. Why did David want the ark in Jerusalem? Because it symbolized God's presence in the midst of His people. In fact, it was the very place where God dwelt with His own. The most dishonoring thing that could have happened to Israel was for the ark to be captured by heathen enemies.

You may ask, "What does this have to do with our subject? How does it speak of Christ in the Old Testament Scriptures?" Just as the ark of the covenant in the holy of holies was the dwelling place of God among Israel, so the church is the dwelling place of God with His people in this age. Oh, I'm not speaking of a building, an edifice, but rather the church, which is the body of Christ. Paul wrote,

> Now, therefore, ye are no more strangers and
> sojourners, but fellow citizens with the saints,
> and of the household of God;

And are built upon the foundation of the apostles
and prophets, Jesus Christ Himself being the chief
cornerstone,
In whom all the building fitly framed together
groweth unto an holy temple in the Lord;
In whom ye also are built together for an
habitation of God through the Spirit
(Ephesians 2:19-22).

As you read the first few chapters of Acts, you see a
risen, glorified, immortal Savior communing with mor-
tals. For 40 days He was with them, then He led His disciples out to Bethany and told them,
But ye shall receive power, after the Holy Spirit is
come upon you; and ye shall be witnesses unto
Me both in Jerusalem, and in all Judea, and in
Samaria, and unto the uttermost part of the earth
(Acts 1:8).

No instruction like this can be found in all the Old
Testament! Pentecost followed Christ's ascension, and
the changes were noted immediately. On that day they
were all Jews, and they witnessed first to the Jews,
with 3,000 being converted. Persecution followed.
Peter was sent to the Gentiles. Converted Jews began
to fraternize with previously hated Gentiles. These
new believers, Jew and Gentile, forsook the temple and
met in houses. They discarded the elaborate rituals,
replacing them with the simple ordinances. They set
aside the sabbath day in favor of Sunday, the Lord's
Day. Why? Because the ascended Lord Jesus had sent
the Holy Spirit to dwell within them, and they were carrying out His word.

DAVID'S FAILURE
What has happened to the church in the intervening
centuries? David's failure to handle the ark correctly,
as recorded in 1 Chronicles 13, is a picture of the
church's failure today. Consider these points:
1. David consulted men rather than God's Word
(13:1). The New Testament commands that we are not
to be menpleasers, but "the servants of Christ, doing
the will of God from the heart" (Ephesians 6:6).

2. David was popular with the people. "All the congregation said that they would do so; for the thing was right in the eyes of all the people" (v. 4). Popularity often wrecks both men and churches. The works of the flesh never get a single convert. The church of the Lord Jesus Christ will never impress the world by becoming worldly (James 4:4).

3. David used human methods instead of God's plans. The Lord had given plain instructions for transporting the ark. The tribe of Levi was set aside for tabernacle service, and they were to bear the ark by means of staves that fit through rings fastened to its side. There was no place for wheels. Yet David used an ox cart, like those used by the Philistines. Likewise, the church cannot be driven by artificial means or worldly methods. All sorts of gimmicks are used in the Lord's work today. But God has ordained that men are to be saved through "the foolishness of preaching." "Faith cometh by hearing, and hearing by the word of God" (Romans 10:17). Substituting human efforts for God's way will always bring disaster.

4. The tragedy of the affair. Everything seemed to be going right. There was music and dancing, a new cart, and oxen. The cart got as far as the threshing floor, and then the animals stumbled. Uzza, a man not appointed of God to carry the ark, reached out to steady it. God smote him dead! Poor fellow, he actually thought he was doing a service to God. Evidently no one had instructed him. He was doing what he was told, and now he was dead. How sad—yet it's happening today! The church is filled with men and women who think they are doing God a service, while indeed they are "dead in trespasses and sins." It's a travesty upon divine grace and order to get people to serve the Lord when they are either unconverted or carnal Christians working in their own strength.

For 3 months the ark was stored in the residence of Obed-edom. The glory of God was hidden in a house! No sign of God's presence could be found in Israel. Everything was dead and cold, just like the Philistines. But the house of Obed-edom was greatly blessed. When the presence of God is experienced in the life of an individual, His rich blessings always abound.

The sequel to this story is found in 1 Chronicles 15, when David finally did things God's way. The priests and the Levites "sanctified themselves to bring up the ark of the Lord God of Israel" (v. 14). When the ark was safely inside, communion with God was restored.

The secret of an effective, powerful, growing church is to acknowledge the presence of God's Spirit and to obey His leading in every aspect of church life and ministry. God's work must be done God's way.

2 CHRONICLES

This book, a continuation of the story of 1 Chronicles, is confined to the story of the house of David. The emphasis is upon the religious history of David's successors rather than the political occurrences, and it covers a period of more than 400 years. The history focuses upon the temple, beginning with the ascension of Solomon to the throne and ending with desolation and the captivity. In typological teaching, a considerable portion of the book sets forth the millennial reign of Christ on the earth. In this connection we read of silver, atonement money, and also of the altar and the veil.

OUTLINE OF THE BOOK

I. The Reign of Solomon (1-9)

Since nothing is said in 2 Chronicles of Solomon's sensuality, sin, and failure, his reign is a picture of the glorious rule of David's greater Son, the Lord Jesus, in the millennial kingdom.

II. The Rebellion of the Ten Tribes (10)

After Solomon died, his son Rehoboam ascended the throne. A series of foolish decisions led to the dividing of the kingdom. The reuniting of Judah and Israel will take place when Israel is restored. (See Isaiah 11:10-13; Jeremiah 23:5,6; and Ezekiel 37:15-28.)

III. The Kings of Judah (11-36)

The period from Solomon to the Babylonian captivity was characterized by moral declension and apostasy, except for five revivals. It is noteworthy that each of these revivals began at the house of God and with the Word of God. They are:

A. Asa's renewal of the altar (15). The place of sacrifice had fallen into disuse during Asa's father's reign. The word of the Lord through Obed stirred him to restore it.

B. Jehoshaphat's establishment of missions (17). This suggests that the Word of God was not known throughout the kingdom.

C. Joash's repair of the temple for worship (23,24). The place of worship had become dilapidated by misuse and disuse.

D. Hezekiah's opening of the temple for worship (29-31). God's house had been closed under wicked King Ahaz.

E. Josiah's discovery of the "book of the law" (34,35). This demonstrates how sad the spiritual condition of Judah was at that time. The Word of God had been lost in a closed and mutilated temple. It was forgotten until uncovered during repairs.

IV. The Captivity (36:15-23)

Sporadic, temporary revivals do not hold the people for God. The patience of God with His people at last came to an end. The book begins with the splendor of Solomon and closes with the devastating captivity of Israel. This illustrates that the very best that man can achieve in his own strength is doomed to failure.

SOME BRIGHT SPOTS

The revivals were encouraging interludes in Judah's history, and one of these is reported in chapter 34. Josiah longed for fellowship with God. He was not particularly following David's example, or Hezekiah's, but he sought "the God of David." As a result of this choice, there were 4 years of silence, study, devotion, and prayer. The law of cause and effect was at work here. The nearer he got to God, the more his eyes were opened to the idolatry of Judah. When Isaiah saw the Lord, he said, "Send me" (6:8). Likewise, after Josiah found God, he was willing to work for the Lord.

While cleaning the temple, the workmen made a remarkable discovery. They found a copy of the law of Moses that had been lost right in the temple! This was the very place it was supposed to be displayed and read. When the Bible is neglected, idolatry of some form always develops.

When the sacred writings were read in the presence of Josiah, he tore his clothes in conviction of sin. He then initiated sweeping reforms throughout the kingdom. The worship of God, including the celebration of the passover, was resumed.

Illumination comes through recognition of duty and obedience to God. "I being in the way, the Lord led me ..." (Genesis 24:27). God revealed the coming judgment to Josiah upon Judah (2 Chronicles 34:24-28). The only remedy for apostasy is judgment.

MESSIANIC NOTE

Speaking of Himself, our Lord said to the scribes and Pharisees, "Behold, a greater than Solomon is here" (Matthew 12:42). The coming earthly reign of the Lord Jesus Christ will far outshine the riches and glory of Solomon's day.

EZRA

The book of Ezra is named for its author, one of its principal characters, and covers a period of about 80 years. It is one of six post-captivity books, joined by Nehemiah, Esther, Haggai, Zechariah, and Malachi. We are told in 2 Chronicles 36:19, 20 that the king of the Chaldeans (Babylonians) "burned the house of God, and broke down the wall of Jerusalem, and burned all its palaces with fire, and destroyed all its precious vessels. And those who had escaped from the sword carried he away to Babylon, where they were servants to him and his sons until the reign of the kingdom of Persia."

As the book of Ezra opens, 70 years have elapsed since the captivity began. Persia has followed Babylon in world dominion, and Cyrus is upon the throne. He learns by reading the prophecy of Isaiah (Isaiah 44:28; 45:1,2) that he is the one who is to see that Jerusalem and the temple are rebuilt. Cyrus issues a proclamation; a company of volunteers from among the exiles returns to the city of Jerusalem, led by Zerubbabel. They build an altar, offer sacrifices, and begin to construct a temple. Although the effort is met with fierce opposition and resulting delays, the temple is finally finished and dedicated.

Some 50 years later, Ezra the scribe leads a second company of people back to Jerusalem, bringing the golden vessels that Nebuchadnezzar had taken. When he learns that the Jews have intermarried, he calls upon them to confess their sins and put away their foreign wives. Ezra's name means "help." The theme of the book is found in this key verse: " . . . to build the house of the Lord which is in Jerusalem" (Ezra 1:5).

But does this book speak of Christ, and does Christ speak to us in this book? Indeed, a number of lessons emerge from the book of Ezra, and we shall consider several of them.

THE IMMUTABILITY OF GOD'S WORD

Henry Drummond said, "The only stable thing in the universe is the law of nature." But behind nature's law stands the God who made it. And His Book, the Bible, is just as immutable as He is. "Forever, O Lord, Thy word is settled in heaven" (Psalm 119:89). What an example of this is found in the book of Ezra!

Approximately 170 years beforehand, Isaiah had written, "Who saith of Cyrus, He is My shepherd, and shall perform all My pleasure; even saying to Jerusalem, Thou shalt be built; and to the temple, Thy foundation shall be laid" (Isaiah 44:28). Isaiah records this further word of Jehovah about Cyrus, "I will direct all his ways; he shall build My city, and he shall let go My captives" (Isaiah 45:13). When we read the context of this chapter, we see clearly that Jehovah was speaking of Cyrus. Very possibly, Daniel had given the scroll of Isaiah or Jeremiah to the king. Remember, God sets into motion the machinery of nations in order to carry out His will.

Mark it well, whatever God's prophets predict will surely come to pass. God's promises will be fulfilled, not figuratively nor allegorically, but exactly and literally.

OPPOSITION TO GOD'S WORK

Opposition from three sides sprang up when Zerubbabel started to build the temple. First was the opposition of the pessimists (Ezra 3:10-13). We read that "fear was upon them because of the people of those countries" (3:3). How like folks today! Even though we acknowledge a creeping apostasy in Christendom, this does not mean that we have to give in to it. Some Christians are zealous and holy, while others are carnal and mistaught. Surrounded as we are by spiritual decline, we are given courage when we consider how faithfully God keeps His Word.

The second form of opposition which the workers experienced was cooperation (4:1-3). The adversaries wanted to join in and help the Jews build the temple. How subtle the work of Satan! The answer from Zerubbabel and the leaders was firm, "Ye have nothing to do with us to build an house unto our God; but we ourselves together will build unto the Lord God of Israel" (4:3). The opposition hired counselors and lawyers to write letters back to Babylon, leveling charges against the builders. Soon a directive came from the king ordering the work to stop. At this point God raised up two prophets, Haggai and Zechariah, whose encouragement caused Zerubbabel and Jeshua to begin again the work God had sent them to do.

The third form of opposition was a call to compromise. This is a standard trick of Satan. When he cannot beat down a work of God by force, he offers compromise. This is exactly what happened. The people of Israel, the priests, and the Levites had taken daughters of the heathen nations surrounding Jerusalem as wives for their sons. So "the holy seed have mixed themselves with the people of those lands" (9:2). When Ezra found out about it, he tore his garments and fell upon his knees and began to pray. His prayer will give you a sense of real confession of sin (see Ezra 9:5-15). Chapter 10 lists those who came to confess and offer sacrifice: 17 priests, 6 Levites, 4 singers and porters, and 86 others.

CHRIST'S WORD TO SINNERS

Some of the principles in this account are reiterated in the New Testament and authenticated by the word of Christ. Consider the example that follows.

Before the returning remnant could begin any work, they had to erect an altar and offer sacrifices. This is always the starting place, as the author of Hebrews points out. "And almost all things are by the law purged with blood, and without shedding of blood is no remission" (Hebrews 9:22). No works are acceptable to God until a sacrifice for sin has first been appropriated. In fact, not only are good works of no help unless sins are forgiven, they are a hindrance.

The names of all those who had sinned were written down (Ezra 10:18-24). God is still keeping records. Man must not trifle with God, lest as Andrew Bonar, the old Scottish preacher, wrote, "He awaits the terror of his doom, the judgment and the pain."

TYPICAL TEACHING

The return of the remnant from Babylon is a faint picture of the return of Israel from worldwide dispersion. For "in his days Judah shall be saved, and Israel shall dwell safely; and this is His name whereby He shall be called, THE LORD OUR RIGHTEOUSNESS. Therefore, behold, the days come, saith the Lord, that they shall no more say, The Lord liveth, who brought up the children of Israel out of the land of Egypt, but, The Lord liveth, who brought up and who led the seed of the house of Israel out of the north country, and from all countries to which I had driven them, and they shall dwell in their own land" (Jeremiah 23:6-8).

In like manner, the rebuilding of the temple foreshadows that millennial temple which Ezekiel said will be erected in Jerusalem (see Ezekiel 40-48). The keeping of the feasts by the remnant that returned under the decree of Cyrus speaks typically of the future time when restored Israel will keep the feast of tabernacles in the millennial age. Zechariah spoke of that time, saying, "And it shall come to pass that everyone that is left of all the nations which came against Jerusalem shall even go up from year to year to worship the King, the Lord of hosts, and to keep the feast of tabernacles" (Zechariah 14:16). Seated upon that throne will be David's greater Son, the Lord Jesus Christ.

NEHEMIAH

Fourteen years after Ezra led his company back to Jerusalem, Nehemiah, servant to the king of Persia, heard sad news about the holy city. He wept, prayed, and fasted, and then was questioned by Artaxerxes the king. Nehemiah asked the ruler to send him to Jerusalem so that he might rebuild the walls. When the king responded affirmatively, Nehemiah journeyed to the beloved city. At night, by himself, he surveyed the walls of Jerusalem. He found them broken down and saw that the gates had been consumed with fire. So he rallied the people and started to rebuild the walls.

The book of Nehemiah covers about 11 years of Israel's history. Ezra built the temple—which should always come first. Nehemiah built the walls and the city—and this should follow. The name Ezra means "help" or "saving help"; Nehemiah means "comfort." Jesus Christ came to be the saving help of His people; the Holy Spirit came as the Comforter to guide and strengthen His people.

All Scripture was given by the inspiration of God. "The testimony of Jesus is the spirit of prophecy" (Revelation 19:10). Since this is the case, then what message does the Lord Jesus have for us in the book of Nehemiah? Just as Nehemiah was the one who restored the walls of Jerusalem and the morals of his people, so the Lord Jesus Christ will be the One who restores the nation of Israel. This promise of the Lord is sure: "And I will shake all nations, and the desire of all nations shall come; and I will fill this house with glory, saith the Lord of hosts" (Haggai 2:7). Not only were the temple and the walls of Jerusalem restored, but the nation itself will someday experience rebirth under the Messiah, the Lord Jesus Christ.

The theme of Nehemiah is set forth in this verse: "The God of heaven will prosper us; therefore we, His servants, will arise and build" (Nehemiah 2:20).

OUTLINE OF THE BOOK

    I. Return and Repair (1-7)
    II. Repentance and Revival (8-10)
    III. Settlement and Separation (11-13)

The entire book presents in typology two events of the last days: (1) the restoration of civil government to the Jews, and (2) their national supremacy in the millennial age.

TYPICAL TEACHING OF THE GATES

Chapter 3 of Nehemiah contains the record of the rebuilding of the gates in the wall around Jerusalem. How wonderfully these gates portray the work of Christ for and in the believer! Ten gates were restored in all, and we will consider the meaning of each.

1. *The Sheep Gate* (3:1). This was the gate of sacrifice, which is always the starting point in the life of the believer. The apostle Paul said, "For I delivered unto you first of all that which I also received, that Christ died for our sins according to the scriptures . . ." (1 Corinthians 15:3). Revelation 5 depicts a graphic scene in heaven, when four living creatures and the twenty-four elders fall down before the Lamb. They sing "a new song, saying, Thou art worthy to take the scroll, and to open its seals; for Thou wast slain, and hast redeemed us to God by Thy blood out of every kindred, and

tongue, and people, and nation" (Revelation 5:9). God's great work for time and eternity centers in the sacrifice of His Son, the Lamb of God, at Calvary.

2. *The Fish Gate* (v. 3). Having received salvation through the sacrifice of Christ, we are to become fishers of men (Matthew 4:19).

3. *The Old Gate* (v. 6). Every believer is to stay with the old paths, affirming and practicing the "faith which was once delivered unto the saints" (Jude 3).

4. *The Valley Gate* (v. 13). Humility is to be a trait of every follower of Christ. "Let this mind be in you, which was also in Christ Jesus..." (Philippians 2:5-8).

5. *The Dung Gate* (v. 14). This was the place where refuse was cast out of the city. Every Christian needs a "garbage dump." The apostle Paul had one, for he wrote these words to the Philippians: "Yea doubtless, and I count all things but loss for the excellency of the knowledge of Christ Jesus, my Lord; for whom I have suffered the loss of all things, and do count them but refuse, that I may win Christ, and be found in Him, not having mine own righteousness, which is of the law, but that which is through the faith of Christ, the righteousness which is of God by faith" (Philippians 3:8,9).

6. *The Fountain Gate* (v. 15). This gate speaks of the overflowing life, the "rivers of living water" made possible by the Holy Spirit (John 7:38).

7. *The Water Gate* (v. 26). Interestingly, this gate did not need repair. Water is a type of the Word of God. His Word never needs repair, for it is pure, refreshing, enduring. "Christ also loved the church, and gave Himself for it, that He might sanctify and cleanse it with the washing of water by the word" (Ephesians 5:25,26).

8. *The Horse Gate* (v. 28). The horse in Scripture often speaks of war. Christians are in a continual warfare. God has provided sufficient equipment—the panoply of power, the full armor described in Ephesians 6:10-18.

9. *The East Gate* (v. 29). This was the gate through which the shekinah glory left Israel (Ezekiel 10). When that transcendent glory returns, it will also be from the east. "And, behold, the glory of the God of

Israel came from the way of the east; and His voice was like a noise of many waters, and the earth shined with His glory" (Ezekiel 43:2). The east gate therefore speaks of the return of our Lord to this earth. When He comes again, His feet will stand upon the Mount of Olives (Zechariah 14:4).

10. *The Hammiphkad Gate* (v. 31). The Hebrew word signifies judgment. How suggestive this is of the judgments that await this earth and all who live upon it! The nations of the world will be summoned to judgment in the valley of Megiddo.

ENEMIES OF THE WORK

Such a magnificent work for God as Nehemiah and his co-laborers were engaged in is never finished without interference from the enemy. Three conspirators opposed Nehemiah, and they are representative of the present-day enemies of the gospel.

1. *Sanballat.* This man's name means "hate in disguise." He represents the wisdom of this world and its opposition to Christ and His gospel. Most organized religion hates Jesus Christ. Paul spoke of it as being a form of deception when he said, "And no marvel; for Satan himself is transformed into an angel of light. Therefore, it is no great thing if his ministers also be transformed as the ministers of righteousness, whose end shall be according to their works" (2 Corinthians 11:14,15).

2. *Tobiah.* His name means "the servant," or possibly, "the Lord is good." He is a representative of those who make a formal profession of faith. They have a good name but a bad heart. This man Tobiah was a sort of puppet for his master Sanballat.

3. *Geshem.* This man's name means "a violent shower." In the case of Nehemiah and his workers, he brought a shower of ridicule and criticism. Geshem was an Arabian, a descendant of Ishmael.

PRACTICAL TRUTHS

God blessed the labors of Nehemiah and the Israelites for a number of reasons. The people "had a mind to work" (4:6). Nehemiah and his men watched and prayed. "We made our prayer . . . and set a watch" (4:9). Each man knew his work and stayed with it. How vital for Christians to recognize their gifts and to exercise them. Not only did they work with their hands in rebuilding the wall but they also had on their armor, the weapons of warfare. "Everyone with one of his hands wrought in the work, and with the other hand held a weapon" (4:17).

This was the exercise of faith, for "without faith it is impossible to please Him" (Hebrews 11:6). G. Campbell Morgan suggests that "The life of faith is sure of God; acts with Him and for Him; declines all compromise and trusts God."

ESTHER

The book of Esther is one of the most beautiful stories in all of literature. Even though the name of God is not mentioned in it, no book of the Bible teaches His providence more forcefully. The book covers a period of about 12 years, falling somewhere between the events recorded in the sixth and seventh chapters of Ezra. The setting is the court of Xerxes, the king of Persia. The Bible refers to him as Ahasuerus. At this period in history, a great number of Jews were still living in Persia.

OUTLINE OF THE BOOK

    I. Haman's Ascendancy (1-5)
       Haman was the enemy of the Jews and sought their extinction.

    II. Mordecai's Ascendancy (6-10).
       Mordecai was concerned for the welfare of his people, the Jews.

The record of Luke 24, particularly the journey of the risen Christ with the two disciples to Emmaus, states that "beginning at Moses and all the prophets, He expounded unto them, *in all the scriptures,* the things concerning Himself" (Luke 24:27). Where in the book of Esther, this book without the mention of God's name, do we find teachings about Christ?

I recommend that you read again the entire book to refresh your mind about the historical account. Before we consider where Christ is found in the book of Esther, we will consider some practical matters.

THE PROVIDENCE OF GOD

An unseen hand is at work behind all human affairs. Who shapes the destinies of nations—politicians? Never! As a lad, I was fascinated by the operation of a certain machine in the Union Station in Pittsburgh. As we waited for an arriving train, we would stand at the desk in the ticket office and watch a machine with an electric pen attached. A roll of paper was located beneath that pen, and periodically it would begin to write. Some miles distant, somewhere up the line of the Pennsylvania Railroad, a stationmaster or yardmaster would be writing down the position of trains and their time of arrival on a similar scroll. The corresponding electric pen in the station would move in the exact handwriting of the originator. I was always amazed at that apparatus.

Similarly, the providential hand of an Almighty God is behind the destiny of nations. James Russell Lowell wrote, "Truth forever on the scaffold,/ Wrong forever on the throne;/ But that scaffold sways the future,/ And behind the dim unknown/ Standeth God amid the shadows,/ Keeping watch upon His own."

All things move by the knowledge of Almighty God and according to His ordained plan and purpose. The book of Esther is a confirmation of Psalm 11:4, "The Lord is in His holy temple, the Lord's throne is in heaven; His eyes behold, His eyelids test the children of men." Woven into God's plans are the most minute details of human history. This is illustrated in the turn of events of the story of Esther. The rejection of a Gentile queen, the choice of Esther, and the finding of the records led finally to the exaltation of Mordecai and the sparing of the Jewish race.

Providence is not blind fate. The word "providence" means, "foresight coupled with activity." God alone is able to act on the basis of foreknowledge. The book of Esther sets forth two great doctrines: man's free will and God's absolute sovereignty. Both are at work here. Haman made his plans and Mordecai was busy with his political maneuvering, yet all was done within the boundaries of God's direction.

THE FATE OF THE WICKED

Another very practical lesson to be gained from the book of Esther is that the prosperity of the wicked is unsafe and unsatisfying, and that it ends in adversity. The experience of the psalmist is recorded as follows: "For I was envious of the foolish, when I saw the prosperity of the wicked" (Psalm 73:3). But then he continued in verses 16 and 17, "When I thought to know this, it was too painful for me, until I went into the sanctuary of God; then understood I their end."

We often see the adversity of the good alongside the prosperity of the wicked. We would tend to ask why, but the book of Esther shows us clearly that the trial of faith results in final victory for the righteous.

DISPENSATIONAL TEACHING

The book of Esther presents us with a picture of God's current relationship with the Jews. The Jewish people as a whole have been out of their land for 1900 years. During this time they have been under many Gentile rulers. Satan repeatedly has had a "Haman" planning their destruction. But all along, God has been in the shadows watching over His covenant people Israel. Even though in their present unbelief they may refuse to recognize His hand, He continues His watchful care over His ancient people.

THE MESSIANIC PLAN

Haman, the Jew-hater from the cursed seed of Amalek, is a picture of the wicked one who will arise in the endtime of this age and seek the extermination of Israel. The "man of sin [will] be revealed, the son of perdition, who opposeth and exalteth himself above all that is called God, or that is worshiped, so that he, as God, sitteth in the temple of God, showing himself that he is God" (2 Thessalonians 2:3,4). Just as Haman's end came by decree of the king, so Antichrist, the man of sin, will be destroyed by God's King, the Lord Jesus Christ. Haman was hanged on the gallows; the man of sin will be cast into the lake of fire.

It appears to me that Esther foreshadows that faithful Jewish remnant in the days of the tribulation. Notice an expression that appears in chapter 5, verse 1, "Now it came to pass on the *third day....*" How beautifully this ties in with the prophecy of Hosea, "After two days will He revive us; in the third day He will raise us up, and we shall live in His sight" (Hosea 6:2). This speaks of the national resurrection of the remnant of Israel in the last days. Esther's Jewish name was Hadassah, meaning "myrtle." Afterward it was changed to Esther, meaning "a star." This signifies what will happen to that nation in the future. God will take the remnant of believing Israel out of great suffering and trial and bring the nation to the place of exaltation.

Mordecai stands out as a figure of the Lord Jesus. He was a despised Jew for whom a scaffold was built. The same scaffold proved to be the undoing of his enemy, and Mordecai was exalted to the throne. How forcefully this speaks of Him who is greater than Mordecai, and who will bring peace to His earthly people and the nations of the world. Mordecai was the revealer of secrets. In Christ are hidden all the secrets of wisdom and knowledge, and He "of God is made unto us wisdom, and righteousness, and sanctification, and redemption" (1 Corinthians 1:30). Mordecai was elevated to the throne. He delivered Israel and was next in authority to the king. By the wonder-working providence and grace of Jehovah, salvation was interposed on behalf of the nation and the world.

Yes, the story of Christ is foreshadowed once again in the Old Testament in the account of Esther.

JOB

Job is classified as one of the poetical books of the Old Testament. It may be the most ancient of the Bible writings. That such a man really lived is sufficiently proved by the testimony of the Holy Spirit in Ezekiel 14:14,20 and James 5:11 where his name is mentioned. Job lived in the time of the patriarchs, probably long before the days of Moses. He offered sacrifices on behalf of his family, and no reference is made in Job to the book of the law given from Sinai. Another indication of the early writing of the book is the fact that Job lived to be approximately 210 years of age.

No other Bible book contains as much scientific truth as Job. Consider, for example, the passage that says God "hangeth the earth upon nothing" (26:7). Job's contemporaries all believed that the earth was flat, and that it rested on the shoulders of one of the gods or the back of an elephant or giant sea turtle. Think of it! Startlingly accurate scientific statements written more than 3,000 years before the discovery of America!

We may well write over the entire book the word "tested." Job's name means "persecuted." The theme of the book sounds forth loud and clear: "He knoweth the way that I take; when He hath tested me, I shall come forth as gold" (Job 23:10).

OUTLINE OF THE BOOK

 I. Prolog (1:1-2:8): A look behind the scenes.
 II. Job and His Wife (2:9,10)
 III. Job and His Three Friends (2:11-31:40)
 IV. Job and Elihu (32-34)
 V. Jehovah and Job (38-41)
 VI. Job's Final Answer (42:1-6)
 VII. Epilog (42:7-17)

The overriding question in the book of Job is this: "Why do the godly suffer?"

FOUR DIFFERENT ANSWERS

The above question is answered in the book of Job from four principal and divergent viewpoints. We will consider these representative opinions about why people suffer.

1. *Satan's view.* Satan hurled the challenge into the face of God that His people love and serve Him only to gain temporal advantage. Hear the adversary say, "Doth Job fear God for nothing?" (Job 1:9). God named that evil insinuation the devil's lie. In effect, God said to Satan, "There are men on earth who will follow me in poverty." The record tells us that Job fell down upon the ground and worshiped God, saying, "Naked came I out of my mother's womb, and naked shall I return there. The Lord gave, and the Lord hath taken away; blessed be the name of the Lord" (1:21). But God went beyond this to prove to Satan that there are men on earth who will trust Him even while their bodies are wracked with pain and disease (see Job's remarks in 2:7-10). We must note this: it often takes more faith to suffer than it does to be healed. God places that faith just as high on the scroll as any other. Look again at Hebrews 11:1 through 34, then read carefully verses 35-39. Yes, God does honor suffering faith.

2. *The view of Eliphaz, Bildad, and Zophar.* These three friends of Job came to the conclusion that the suf-

fering of the righteous is punishment for known, but perhaps secret, sins. This viewpoint is refuted by God's Word and the experience of Job. Eliphaz expressed his opinion that suffering is punishment for sin in these words: "Remember, I pray thee, who ever perished, being innocent? Or where were the righteous cut off?" (Job 4:7). Be assured of this: not all of "Job's comforters" are dead. A pernicious doctrine that is extant today says that sickness is always the result of sin or that people don't get well because they lack faith. People who believe this do not understand the book of Job.

3. *The view of Elihu.* This wise man pictured God as a great God. He gave us a noble and true accounting of man and suffering. But Elihu was conceited, and he was guilty of the very thing of which he accused Job.

4. *God's view.* God finally confronted Job and, in a unique revelation of Himself, gave him a discourse on His attributes. In his response, Job expressed God's solution to the problem of human suffering in his own words (42:1-6). They could be summed up this way: The godly are afflicted so that they may be brought to self-knowledge and self-judgment. Afflictions are purifying. Job was a good man, but he was self-righteous. The book of Job is a picture of the situation that is stated in 1 Corinthians 11:13,32; Luke 22:31,32; and 1 Corinthians 5:5.

THE LORD JESUS IN THE BOOK

Job longed for a mediator (9:32,33). The word translated "daysman" in verse 33 means "mediator." He realized that he was a fallen man, the offspring of Adam. He knew that in heaven was a holy God and that between him and God was a vast gulf. His cry was for a kinsman-redeemer, and by faith he saw the God-man. "For there is one God, and one mediator between God and men, the man, Christ Jesus" (1 Timothy 2:5).

Job's vision of a future life had been obscure, as witnessed by his question, "If a man die, shall he live again?" (Job 14:14). But light broke upon his soul, for later we hear him exclaim, "For I know that my Redeemer liveth, and that He shall stand at the latter day upon the earth; and though after my skin worms destroy this body, yet in my flesh shall I see God" (19:25,26). Job understood the process of bodily disintegration, but with the eye of faith he also saw the resurrection and his Redeemer standing upon this earth. He saw himself in a future body of flesh, for he said of Christ, "Whom I shall see for myself, and mine eyes shall behold, and not another" (v. 27).

Yes, this is just one more proof of the validity of our Lord's words, "They ... testify of Me" (John 5:39).

A PRACTICAL THOUGHT

A right view of God, a right view of self, and then a right view of others is the correct order. The blessings described in Job 42:10 were the result of a vision of God that followed with an abhorrence of self, tears of repentance, the sweet odor of burnt offering, and the embrace of love (42:11).

PSALMS

Next in the order of the canon of Scripture is the best-known book in the Bible, the Psalms. The Hebrew title means "the book of praises." The predominant thought of the book is expressed by the word "worship," a term that means "prostration." This kind of worship recognizes both the supremacy of God and our place of submission as worshipers. What a remarkable collection of inspired writings is found in the book of Psalms!

Edward Irving wrote, "Every angel of joy and of sorrow wept as he passed over David's heart; and the hearts of 100 men strove and struggled together within the narrow continent of his single heart." And James H. Brooks said that the Psalms "describe so largely in prophecy the inner life of the Lord Jesus Christ, who was in all points tempted like as we are, yet without sin; and unless that fact is kept constantly in view, the Psalms cannot be read intelligently."

Many of the psalms were written by David himself. At least one is said definitely to be a "prayer of Moses" (Psalm 90). Some were penned by Asaph, the chief musician in David's choir.

DIVISIONS OF THE BOOK

Although there is usually no connection between one

psalm and another, the Psalms were divided into five books by the Hebrews. Each ends with "amen" or "hallelujah."

Psalms 1-41: Davidic Psalms
Psalms 42-72: Levitical Psalms
Psalms 73-89: Psalms of the Time of Hezekiah
Psalms 90-106: Pre-captivity Psalms
Psalms 107-150: Post-captivity Psalms

As with the book of Job, the Psalms were not written as a treatise on science. But when they speak about scientific matters, they are not only accurate but years ahead of their time.

Two-thirds of all the Old Testament quotations made by our Lord and His apostles were from the Psalms. No other book of the Old Testament portrays the past, the present, and the future work of our Lord so vividly. Remember, Christ said to the two disciples on the road to Emmaus, ". . . all things must be fulfilled, which were written in the law of Moses, and in the prophets, and in the psalms, concerning Me" (Luke 24:44). It is recorded that "He expounded unto them, in all the scriptures, the things concerning Himself" (Luke 24:27). This most certainly included the Psalms, for they tell of the sufferings of Christ and the glory that would follow. What do the Psalms say about Christ? I suggest to you the following:

Psalm 2. Christ, the Son of God, is depicted as the appointed Ruler, the King of kings. "I will declare the decree: The Lord hath said unto Me, Thou art My Son; this day have I begotten Thee" (v. 7).

Psalm 8. The Son of God becomes the Son of man in order that we might be made the sons of God. Verses 4 and 5 of this psalm are answered in Hebrews 2:9-18.

Psalm 16. Christ's deliverance from death is prophesied here. Verses 10 and 11 find their fulfillment in the death and resurrection of our Lord. These words were quoted by Peter on the day of Pentecost, showing that David was a prophet.

Psalms 22, 23, 24. These songs are examples of

divine inspiration in the arrangement of the Psalms. They are filled with Messianic teaching about the life and ministry of the Lord Jesus. We shall return shortly to these.

Psalm 40. The New Testament counterpart to this psalm is found in the obedience of Christ (read Hebrews 10:5-7). Consider especially verses 7 and 8 of Psalm 40. Notice also verses 1 through 3, which prefigure the experience of Christ as He is brought forth from death by resurrection.

Psalm 69. The humiliation of Christ is shown in verses 4, 8, 9, 12, and 21. These foreshadowings find their fulfillment in Matthew 13:55,56; Matthew 27:33,34; John 2:17; and Romans 15:3.

Psalm 118. This psalm is part of the special passage that was used as a prayer on passover night. It more than likely was sung by the Lord and His disciples at the Lord's supper, as recorded in Matthew 26:30.

Verse 22 of this psalm speaks definitely of our Lord, as proven by Matthew 21:42; Mark 12:10; and Luke 20:17. Christ specifically applied this verse to Himself.

THE SHEPHERD PSALMS (Psalms 22-24)

The New Testament referred to the work of the Lord Jesus Christ as that of a shepherd in three distinct ways. They correspond to Psalms 22, 23, and 24, which present three aspects of our Lord's ministry on earth.

1. *The Good Shepherd* (Psalm 22). The Lord Jesus made this key statement about Himself: "I am the good shepherd; the good shepherd giveth His life for the sheep" (John 10:11). As you read Psalm 22, you can see a picture of the Lord Jesus, who is the Good Shepherd. In your mind's eye, you are immediately transported to Calvary. The very first verse of Psalm 22 reads, "My God, My God, why hast Thou forsaken Me?" These words were spoken by our Lord from the cross a thousand years later. James M. Gray said, "In the gospels we read of what He said and did, and what was done to Him; in the Psalms we find how He felt and lived in the presence of God."

In verses 7 and 8 of Psalm 22 you can almost hear the taunting of the crowd, the scorn of the people, and the words they hurled at the Savior on the cross. Verse 16 graphically and accurately describes crucifixion, the means of capital punishment used by the Romans. This mode was unknown to the Jews of David's day. Verse 18 records prophetically that the soldiers would divide the dying Messiah's garments among themselves, casting lots for them. The latter part of the psalm is marked by a jubilance which portrays the glory of the salvation purchased through the affliction that is so graphically described. The resurrection is not mentioned, but the Sufferer has been delivered and His people will experience indescribable blessing because of what He has done (vv. 22-31). The closing verses describe the universal nature of this blessing: it will extend down through coming generations. The very last phrase, "that He hath done," is seen by some as a reference to the fact that on the cross our Lord could say, "It is finished." Thus Psalm 22 is the crucifixion psalm. The Good Shepherd has given His life for the sheep.

2. *The Great Shepherd* (Psalm 23). What tender emotions and thoughts of praise fill our hearts as we read Psalm 23! This is not a song about a dying or a dead shepherd, but of a living and leading One. It is in the present tense; it speaks of today. Christ arose from the dead to be our Great Shepherd. "Now the God of peace, that brought again from the dead our Lord Jesus, that great Shepherd of the sheep, through the blood of the everlasting covenant..." (Hebrews 13:20). Psalm 23 is the story of the present work of Christ. It is not the work of the cross, but of the crook, the curved end of the staff used by the shepherd to lead, to guide, to direct his sheep. It is symbolic of the outstretched hand of the Shepherd in protection of His flock. Psalm 23 is the story of the abiding presence of Christ; it is the psalm of the Great Shepherd.

3. *The Chief Shepherd* (Psalm 24). The apostle Peter wrote, "And when the chief Shepherd shall appear, ye shall receive a crown of glory that fadeth not away"

(1 Peter 5:4). Listen! Someone is coming! Who is it? The King of Glory! Yes, One is coming who has the right to reign, for "the earth is the Lord's, and the fullness thereof; the world, and they who dwell therein" (Psalm 24:1). Psalm 24 is the psalm of the Chief Shepherd, who is coming to rule over the earth. It reminds us of Psalm 2, which is also a psalm of the King of Glory.

Lack of space prevents us from presenting the full scope of the portrayal of Christ in the Psalms. I suggest that you read the Psalms reverently, meditating and rejoicing in the glory of Christ reflected in this glorious "book of praises."

PROVERBS

Proverbs is the third of the poetical books of the Old Testament. Someone has termed it a book of "laws from heaven for life on earth." Proverbs is one of the three volumes of "wisdom literature" of the ancient Hebrews.

The first nine chapters are instructions by Solomon to his son—a series of parental admonitions about seeking wisdom and shunning folly. In the remaining chapters are 374 maxims that touch every phase of life.

The divine origin of the book is attested to by the fact that after 3,000 years its counsels still stand, undaunted by modern psychology and education.

The keynote of Proverbs is expressed in chapter 1, verse 7, "The fear of the Lord is the beginning of knowledge." That distinguishes this book from all of the wisdom literature of the world. It starts with an affirmation, a fundamental truth, that no educator should ignore. The Hebrew philosophers believed there could be no discovery of ultimate truth apart from revelation. And the revelation with which they began was the existence of God. He filled their vision. Modern philosophy has developed a system that is godless and foolish because there is "no fear of God before their eyes" (Romans 3:18). G. Campbell Morgan wrote that there are two kinds of fear: (1) The fear that God will hurt me, but that is a selfish fear. (2) The fear that I will hurt Him; a fear founded in love and producing holiness of character and righteousness of conduct.

GOD: THE SOURCE OF TRUTH

Our concern in this study is to find where and in what way this book previews Christ. However, let's digress a moment to consider the fear of God as the beginning of all true knowledge. Solomon used a threefold illustration of this in chapter 1. He did so by discussing three spheres of life in which every human being moves.

1. *The Home* (vv. 8,9). "My son, hear the instruction of thy father, and forsake not the law of thy mother; for they shall be an ornament of grace unto thy head, and chains about thy neck." The responsibility of the father and mother is taken for granted. God's first and primary unit of society is the home. A child is unable to understand much about the Infinite. But the child does (or should) see God in his father and mother. Your first impression of God was no doubt made through your father: his laws, his authority, his punishments, his exactness. In your mother's love, devotion, sacrifice, and suffering you saw something of the love and compassion of God. Yes, the fear of God starts in the home.

2. *Friendships* (v. 10). "My son, if sinners entice thee, consent thou not." The circle widens to the period of choosing friendships. The day comes when the child has to make his own choices. A list of those who want comradeship on the basis of self-interest and unscrupulous means is given in Proverbs 1:11-19. The importance of this cycle of life is immeasurable. Let me ask you: Are you choosing your friendships on the basis of the knowledge gained by the fear of God?

3. *The Business World* (vv. 20,21). "Wisdom crieth outside; she uttereth her voice in the streets; she crieth in the chief place of concourse, in the openings of the gates; in the city she uttereth her words." The one who was a child just a few years earlier has now entered the bustle of the busy city. He's in the world of business and commerce. The writer of Proverbs does not say to that one, "Don't go." It is inevitable that the child will

grow and develop and become an adult, entering the everyday world of activity. But this book tells him *how* to go. Note the instruction given in the words, "Turn you at my reproof; behold, I will pour out my spirit unto you, I will make known my words unto you" (v. 23). This is followed by the assurance of verse 33, "But whoso hearkeneth unto me shall dwell safely, and shall be quiet from fear of evil." This advice is further reinforced by those great and familiar verses of chapter 3: "Trust in the Lord with all thine heart, and lean not unto thine own understanding. In all thy ways acknowledge Him, and He shall direct thy paths" (vv. 5,6).

You may well say, "All that is good advice. But how can I follow it if I didn't come from a Christian home, if my companions are not Christians, and if I live under adverse circumstances?" The answers are to be found in chapter 30, which delineates the way of wisdom.

THE PATH OF WISDOM

Let us now look closely at Proverbs 30, taking note of several important steps in the path of wisdom. Agur is speaking, and in verse 2 he confesses that he has discovered his helplessness and unworthiness before God. It's the cry of the penitent, "God be merciful to me a sinner." If we are to walk in the path of wisdom, we must acknowledge our own guilt and weakness.

Agur continues that confession in verse 3 by acknowledging that the wisdom of God is above the wisdom of the world. God's wisdom comes by revelation. "For the wisdom of this world is foolishness with God. For it is written, He taketh the wise in their own craftiness" (1 Corinthians 3:19). Even the wisdom of the great civilization of Greece could not answer man's quest for the true meaning of life. The best the philosophers of Athens could do was erect an altar to "the unknown God" (Acts 17:23).

Overwhelmed by the thought of God's greatness and power, and by the distance between man and God, Agur asked a series of penetrating questions (see Proverbs

107

30:4). The patriarch Job had asked similar questions (compare Job 38:4-7).

Verse 4 ends with an electrifying question: "What is His name, and what is His Son's name, if thou canst tell?" God has a Son! "In the beginning was the Word, and the Word was with God, and the Word was God" (John 1:1). Isaiah would prophesy, "For unto us a Child is born, unto us a Son is given, and the government shall be upon His shoulder; and His name shall be called Wonderful, Counselor, The Mighty God, The Everlasting Father, The Prince of Peace" (Isaiah 9:6).

The next step in the path of wisdom appears in verse 5. "Every word of God is pure." Faith rests upon the Word of God. We can cry with the psalmist, "Thy word is true from the beginning" (Psalm 119:160).

The succeeding step, also expressed in verse 5, is a step of trust. "He is a shield unto those who put their trust in Him." Isaiah recorded a great promise, "Thou wilt keep him in perfect peace, whose mind is stayed on Thee, because he trusteth in Thee" (Isaiah 26:3).

The concluding step in the path of wisdom is expressed in verse 6, "Add thou not unto His words . . . ." The Word of God is our final and complete authority. No man can walk in the path of wisdom without obeying the Word of God.

CHRIST IN PROVERBS

The picture of Christ appears often in Proverbs, for He is the personification of wisdom. James said, "If any of you lack wisdom, let him ask of God, who giveth to all men liberally, and upbraideth not, and it shall be given him" (James 1:5). But it was the apostle Paul in his inspired writings who said, "But unto them who are called, both Jews and Greeks, Christ the power of God, and the wisdom of God" (1 Corinthians 1:24). A little later he said, "But of Him are ye in Christ Jesus, who of God is made unto us wisdom . . ." (v. 30).

Read Proverbs 8:22 through 36 and you will discover the very imprimatur of Christ, the very wisdom of God. "In all thy ways acknowledge Him, and He shall direct thy paths" (Proverbs 3:6).

ECCLESIASTES

The book of Ecclesiastes has been branded as a book of pessimism and denounced by the critics as unworthy of the Holy Spirit's authorship. I must admit that it is indeed filled with hopelessness and despair. Quite often the materialists, the fatalists, and the sensualists support their teachings by sentences lifted from the book of Ecclesiastes.

The opening verse gives the title of the book: "The words of the Preacher, the son of David, king in Jerusalem." The second verse gives the theme of the book: "Vanity of vanities, saith the Preacher, vanity of vanities; all is vanity." But it must be remembered that he speaks only of that which is "under the sun," a phrase that is used 29 times in Ecclesiastes.

This book, given by divine inspiration, is a record of the bitter disappointment that awaits people whose faith soars no higher than the sun. The conclusion a man like that reaches is stated in this key text: "...all was vanity and vexation of spirit, and there was no profit under the sun" (Ecclesiastes 2:11).

C. I. Scofield has written, "It is what man, with the knowledge that there is a holy God and that He will bring everything into judgment, discovers of the emptiness of setting the heart upon things under the sun."

OUTLINE OF THE BOOK

Professor W. G. Moorehead, treating the book as a sermon, gave the following outline:

I. The Text Proved
   A. By experience (1,2)
   B. By observation (3,4)
II. The Text Unfolded
   A. The miseries of life (1:1-2:11)
   B. The hypocrisies of life (2:12-3)
   C. The wrongs and injustices of life (4)
   D. The riches and poverty of life (5)
   E. The uncertainties of life (6-10)
   F. The best thing possible to the natural man apart from God (11:1-12:12)
   G. The best thing possible to the man who knows God and His law (12:13,14)

The man "under the sun" had given himself to studying philosophy and exploring science. He had proved that there is pleasure in imparting happiness. He had tested the power of wine to allay care and sorrow. He had engaged in great works—building houses, planting vineyards, and setting out gardens with pools of water. He had hired servants and maidens, he had sons born in his house, and he gathered great possessions. He employed singers and musicians, and he was crowned with honor and fame. He did all of this—only to find that the ambitions and enjoyments of the world had turned to ashes.

God chose by divine inspiration to preserve in His Word the reasoning of this natural man "under the sun." We will evaluate this man's thinking in the light of God's Word.

A WRONG VIEW OF THE UNIVERSE (1:4-7; 2:24)

As we read this treatise, we must admit that this man had wisdom and was centuries ahead of the scientific minds of his day. He knew the philosophy of the winds and the science of the rainfall—but he saw it only as a great machine. When he looked at himself, he saw another machine and reasoned, "I'm just like the wind and rain; just a drop in the cycles that are ever

110

moving." This wrong view of the universe gave him ...

A WRONG VIEW OF GOD (3:1-9, 18-22)

Perhaps a key to understanding what is being said here is the word that designates God in this passage. The name used is "Elohim," the same word used in the first verse of Genesis. It means "the Strong One," "the Mighty One," "the One far away." The word "Jehovah" is not found in Ecclesiastes. "Jehovah" is the name used to describe God with men, the near name, the name of a covenant-keeping God. The name "Elohim" was used in the creation account, but it was Jehovah who made the coats of skins to clothe Adam and Eve after they had sinned. The man "under the sun" did not see God as the loving Heavenly Father, the covenant-keeping God, the God of redemption.

A RELIGION OF FEAR AND FATALISM (5:1-6)

The whole of this man's religious views is summed up in this statement: "For God is in heaven, and thou upon earth" (5:2). This is the religion of the fatalists who say, "Whatever is to be will be, and there is no use in trying to change it."

AN INDIFFERENT ATTITUDE (7:14-17)

The natural man reasons, "If the faraway God balances things, why shouldn't we do the same?" Therefore, he adopts this attitude: "Don't be too righteous and don't be too wicked." The religious middle-of-the-road philosophy of our day, says, "Do the best you can under the circumstances." This is the thinking of the natural man.

A NARROW VIEW OF LIFE (9:1-6)

The man "under the sun" thought that everyone would share a common fate. He reasoned that one endtime event was in store for all—the righteous and the unrighteous, the good and the evil, the clean and the unclean, the one who sacrifices and the one who does not. His view of life was that the grave ends all. The false religions of our day are quick to quote verse 5. But mark this—this statement is not divine revelation! By God's

111

inspiration these words are included in the Scriptures, but they are the words of a man "under the sun."

What is God's view of life's end? You find it expressed in these words of the apostle Paul: "His own purpose and grace . . . is now made manifest by the appearing of our Savior, Jesus Christ, who hath abolished death, and hath brought life and immortality to light through the gospel" (2 Timothy 1:9,10).

MAKE THE BEST OF THE PRESENT (9:7-10)

The man "under the sun" reasons that he must make the best of every day by eating well, enjoying wine, and making his heart merry. What a picture of the present age! Dress spotlessly; use the most expensive perfumes; live it up! Why? Because a common fate awaits all. But even in the midst of profane hilarity, the natural man is sad. Read carefully the mournful words of Ecclesiastes 9:11 and 12.

THE CLOSING VIEW (12)

After presenting all of this worldly wisdom and natural reasoning, the man "under the sun" gives a personification of old age. The "clouds" are like our sorrows that multiply. The "keepers of the house" are the hands that tremble. The "strong men" are the knees that begin to bow. The "grinders" are the teeth, which become few and can no longer chew strong meat. The "windows" are the eyes that become dim. The "doors" are the ears that can no longer hear the noises of the street. The "silver cord" is the spine that can no longer support the weight. The "golden bowl" is the brain that no longer functions well. The "pitcher" is the heart that becomes diseased. And the "wheel" is the circulation that stops. Then suddenly after this graphic depiction of old age, the man "under the sun" cries out again, "Vanity of vanities, saith the Preacher; all is vanity" (Ecclesiastes 12:8).

CHRIST IN ECCLESIASTES

I could find no better expression of the purpose of this book than that which was written by F. C. Jennings, a

112

devout student of the Word of God. I am quoting from his book *Meditations on Ecclesiastes.*

> No song brightens its pages; no praise is heard amid its exercises. And yet perfectly assured we may be that, listened to aright, it shall speak forth the praise of God's beloved Son; looked at in a right light, it shall set off His beauty. If "He turns the wrath of man to praise Him," surely we may expect no rest from man's sorrows and ignorance. *This, then, we may take it, is the object of the book, to show forth by its dark background the glory of the Lord, to bring into glorious relief against the black cloud of man's need and ignorance the bright light of a perfect, holy revelation;* to let man tell out, in the person of his greatest and wisest, when he too is at the summit of his greatness, with the full advantage of his matured wisdom, the solemn questions of his inmost being; and show that greatness to be of no avail in solving them, that wisdom foiled in the search for their answers (emphasis ours).

The Preacher, Solomon, admonished, "Let us hear the conclusion of the whole matter," and he stated that the best thing for man is to "fear God" and obey Him. At a time when the law was the highest revelation from God, this was a correct conclusion. But it is not the whole duty of man today. Man must take his place before God as a sinner condemned by the law and believe on the Lord Jesus Christ. When he does, he receives life and can live in resurrection power. No preacher of the gospel would ever select Ecclesiastes 12:13,14 as a message of salvation!

Christ is seen in Ecclesiastes in contrast to all that man "under the sun" can reason, achieve, and enjoy. F. C. Jennings said that this book is the contrast between the "new song" and the "old groan." We look beyond the sun to God's Son, and we find in Him an unending source of wisdom and knowledge. The answers to life's deepest questions are bound up in Him.

SONG OF SOLOMON

The Song of Solomon is the closing book of the poetical section of the Old Testament. It is probably censured more and read less than any other book. Critics have said it is indecent, and it may appear to be so to the unspiritual mind. Remember, however, that the Eastern people were a passionate people, both in love and hate.

The highest affection known to man is a husband's love for his wife. Jesus spoke of this devotion when He said, "For this cause shall a man leave father and mother, and shall cleave to his wife, and they two shall be one flesh" (Matthew 19:5).

Some people say that the Song of Solomon is just a love song and therefore has no place in the Bible. A superficial reading of the book might lead to this conclusion. But when you consider the tremendous truth found in Ephesians 5 — that the union of a husband and wife is an earthly illustration of the heavenly relationship between Christ and His church — then the Song of Solomon takes on a new meaning. The child of God sees the love of Christ for His church portrayed through the love of a man for his wife. One of the greatest needs of the church today is a deep, personal love for Christ.

G. Campbell Morgan said, "The song should be treated first as a simple and yet sublime song of human affection. When it is thus understood, reverently the thoughts may be lifted into higher values of setting forth the joys of communion between the spirit of man and the Spirit of God, and ultimately between the church and Christ. Therefore, I can sing the Song of Solomon as setting forth the relationship between Christ and His bride."

The key word of the Song of Solomon is "beloved." The key verse is: "I am my beloved's, and my beloved is mine" (Song of Solomon 6:3). Let us consider the teaching of the book by looking at several important facets of the love-relationship between the bride and the bridegroom.

THE BRIDE'S SELF-KNOWLEDGE (1:5)

The betrothed said of herself, "I am black, but comely." This appears to be a paradox. How can both be possible at the same time? She describes her appearance as black as "the tents of Kedar." Is this not a picture of the human heart? The intense rays of the oriental sun had darkened her (v. 6). But if she exclaims, "I am black," her lover responds, "Thou art all fair, my love; there is no spot in thee" (4:7). Likewise, Christ desires to look upon the church whom He loved so much that He gave Himself for her.

The bride exclaims, "I am . . . comely . . . like the curtains of Solomon" (1:5). What beauty this must have been! Although she did not see much in herself (v. 6), she had a beauty that was not her own. This is a picture of the righteousness of Christ given to the church.

The book contains numerous expressions of mutual affection and admiration. Yet it also has several confessions of failure on the part of the bride. In spite of our shortcomings, the love of the Bridegroom, the Lord Jesus Christ, does not change. The first four chapters of the Song of Solomon show the lovers basking in each other's love. This is like the early church—how she loved her absent Lord!

THE BRIDE'S SLEEP (5:2)

In chapter 5 the mood changes. The bridegroom still loves, but the bride is drowsy. "I sleep, but my heart waketh. It is the voice of my beloved that knocketh" (5:2). Her bridegroom has been out in the night, and his head is wet with dew. He has been gathering precious myrrh. He returns to find her drowsy, so he goes away.

In this present age Christ is away. The risen Lord gave this message to the church at Ephesus: "Thou hast left thy first love" (Revelation 2:4). This may also be translated, "Thou hast ceased loving Me first." Notice the bride's strange condition—she is half-asleep, half-awake. Neither is beneficial. This is a forerunner of the complete sleep.

THE BRIDE'S AWAKENING (5:2)

The bride finally realized that her lover was at the door, but she was too sleepy to open it. He had been diligently working in her behalf, yet she failed to respond to him. Today, Jesus Christ is at the throne of God. He neither slumbers nor sleeps (Psalm 121:4). Night and day He is our Advocate, warding off the accusations of Satan. Were it not for Christ, where would we be? He says to the Father, "I pray for them." And what does He desire of us? The same as He requested of His disciples: "Watch ye and pray, lest ye enter into temptation . . ." (Mark 14:38).

THE BRIDE'S EXCUSES (5:3)

The bride was foolish to say, "I have put off my coat; how shall I put it on? I have washed my feet; how shall I defile them?" (5:3). A backslider usually doesn't need much of an excuse. A very weak alibi serves the purpose when a Christian is out of fellowship with God.

People who are absorbed in the business world, meeting the public, handling thousands of dollars, and engaging in commerce, are often too preoccupied to serve the Lord effectively. The bride had put off her coat and washed her feet. She was concerned only for herself. Why should she be disturbed by a knock? The apostle Paul wrote of some Christians in his day, "For all seek their own, not the things which are Jesus Christ's" (Philippians 2:21).

THE BRIDE'S DISCOVERY (5:6)

"I opened to my beloved" (v. 6). One version translates verse 4, "Her head moved when she saw his hand put in by the hole of the door." But she did not move until "her *heart* was moved" (v. 4). But when she went to open the door, he was already gone. Backsliding always begins with the heart. If there is even a pinhole of disobedience in the door, His searching hand will find it. When she finally responded, he had left. Christ sometimes withholds His blessing so that we will seek Him all the more. Christian, do not trifle with the things of God. "Be not deceived, God is not mocked, for whatever a man soweth, that shall he also reap" (Galatians 6:7).

THE BRIDE'S REMORSE (5:6)

"My soul failed when he spoke." We know that the bridegroom had spoken to her (v. 2). But instead of obeying immediately, she began to make excuses. Now, like Peter would do centuries later, she mournfully remembered her guilt and failure. She knew exactly what the sin was; she had chosen selfish ease over obedience to him. What a miserable condition resulted! (vv. 6-8). First, fellowship was broken. "I sought him, but I could not find him" (v. 6). Sin always leads to separation. When the Spirit of God is grieved, our communion with Christ is interrupted. Please understand—the relationship is not broken, but the fellowship is severed.

Second, her prayer was unanswered. "I called him, but he gave me no answer" (v. 6). Our Lord said, "If ye abide in Me, and My words abide in you, ye shall ask what ye will, and it shall be done unto you" (John 15:7). This requires obedience. No Christian can expect his prayers to be answered if there is disobedience in his life. A striking association is made in the book of James between answers to prayer and the presence of sin. The failure to repent and confess short-circuits the process (James 5:15,16).

Third, the bride lost her testimony. "The watchman that went about the city found me; they smote me, they wounded me; the keepers of the walls took away my veil from me" (5:7). The bride was so changed that the city watchman did not recognize her. Both sorrow and shame came upon her. Likewise, backsliders can expect correction from faithful Christians. Rebuke must be given; repentance and confession are required.

THE BRIDE'S REPENTANCE (5:10-16)

With repentant heart the bride describes her bridegroom. She is not reluctant to acknowledge him now. Following this he returns and their fellowship is restored. She increasingly experiences his deep and unchanging love. At the beginning she could say with an abounding heart, "My beloved is mine, and I am his" (2:16). But now she can declare with complete trust: "I am my beloved's, and his desire is toward me" (7:10).

Across every page of the Song of Solomon could be written these words of the apostle Paul: "This is a great mystery, but I speak concerning Christ and the church" (Ephesians 5:32).

ISAIAH

The careful reader of the sacred Scriptures recognizes immediately that the prophetic books of the Old Testament are not arranged in chronological order. Sixteen "holy men of God" were chosen to speak "as they were moved by the Holy Spirit" (2 Peter 1:21). Their writings come at intervals covering a period of nearly 500 years.

Isaiah, whose name means "salvation of the Lord" or "the Lord will save," is prominently placed at the beginning of the section. He is often called the prophet of redemption.

The prophecies of Isaiah were delivered during the reigns of four kings of Judah: Uzziah, Jotham, Ahaz, and Hezekiah (1:1). He spoke primarily to Judah prior to the exile. In the opening verse he stated that he was about to relate a vision he saw concerning Judah and Jerusalem. He meant precisely that. It was not a vision about the church, but about Judah and Jerusalem. Great principles can be learned from God's dealings with men of old that apply to people in all ages. The mystery of Christ and His church, however, was not revealed to the Old Testament prophets.

One Bible scholar has suggested that chapters 1 through 38 breathe with the Old Testament spirit of judgment and warning, and chapters 40-66 breathe with the New Testament spirit of grace and peace.

OUTLINE OF THE BOOK

Dr. James H. Brooks, noted student and teacher of the

119

Word of God, suggested the following divisions for Isaiah's prophecy:

I. The Sore Punishment of the Jews (1-12)

Though the theme is of harsh judgment, Isaiah also spoke of certain restoration and songs of joy at the second coming of Christ.

II. The Burden of Seven Gentile Nations (13-27)

These people would never have been mentioned by the Spirit except for their connection with God's covenant people. These nations will reappear, though under new names, at the high point of Jewish history, when the promised coming of their Messiah takes place.

III. Israel More Guilty than the Other Nations (28-35)

She would experience God's wrath as a people more advantaged because of her chosen status. The second coming of Christ will end the punishment.

IV. A Historical Interlude (36-39)

This is the third recital of events that occurred during Hezekiah's reign. It presents in type Israel's deadly spiritual sickness, the appearance of Antichrist, and the miraculous deliverance of the Jews, accomplished by the second coming of Christ.

V. God's Controversy with Israel because of Her Idolatry (40-48)

This section contains another promise of the return of Christ, but it ends with these gripping words: "There is no peace, saith the Lord, unto the wicked" (48:22).

VI. God's Sharp Controversy with Israel for Rejecting Christ (49-57)

Once again the section includes a promise of the second coming, but it ends with the harsh words, "There is no peace, saith my God, to the wicked" (57:21).

VII. A Beautiful Description of the Second Coming of Christ (58-66)

Christ will return at the very moment of Israel's worldliness and hypocrisy and defilement. The section ends, however, with this emphatic warning to unbelievers: ". . . their worm shall not die, neither shall their fire be quenched; and they shall be an abhorrence unto all flesh" (66:24).

CHRIST IN ISAIAH: Chapter 6

To give the story of Christ in Isaiah in one brief chapter is nearly impossible. None of the other prophets was permitted to see as much about Christ as Isaiah did. The secret of the whole book is found in chapter 6.

It was the year that King Uzziah died. To get the setting, read 2 Kings 15. Uzziah had been a good ruler, and Isaiah thought very highly of him. But one day "the Lord smote the king, so that he was a leper unto the day of his death, and dwelt in a separate house" (2 Kings 15:5). The prophet Isaiah was dejected. Then came an earthquake, and God permitted him to see One greater than Uzziah. Every child of God needs to catch the vision of what Isaiah saw that day.

1. *His own unworthiness* (Isaiah 6:5). This is the first essential. No one can be of service to the Lord until he comes to the end of himself.

2. *The need of the world* (v. 5). The prophet was devastated when he saw himself and the people of "unclean lips" about him. His eyes were opened to the need of the world.

3. *The sufficiency of Christ* (v. 5). "For mine eyes have seen the King, the Lord of hosts." Isaiah saw the nation in chaos and despair, but he also envisioned God's anointed One upon the throne. Worried because of the death of his beloved king, Isaiah saw beyond the present. How we all need to know that Christ is sufficient in any emergency, under any condition, at any time! The tragedy today is not a defeated Christ but a deluded world and an anemic church. The mists of sin and worldliness have so clouded our vision that we fail to see the enthroned Christ as we really should. Christ said, "All authority is given unto Me in heaven and in earth . . ." (Matthew 28:18). Isaiah said, "I saw also the Lord sitting upon a throne . . ." (6:1), and "I heard the voice of the Lord" (v. 8). What was Isaiah's response to the vision, the cleansing, and the voice?

4. *The appropriate response* (v. 8). "Here am I; send me." He surrendered absolutely to God and His service. I know we cannot standardize the experience of Isaiah and his call to serve, but like conversion, it contains all the necessary elements. The essentials in God's preparation of His man are found here. Someone said, "God prepares a prophet; then He makes the prophet; then He breaks the mold."

5. *The sphere to which he was sent* (vv. 9,10). In an age when we are being told to think positively, Isaiah's assignment seems rather discouraging. He was sent to a people who would hear but not understand, who would see but not perceive, whose heart was fat, whose ears were heavy, and whose eyes were shut. How about today? Perhaps at no time in history has the Christian faced more satanic opposition; never has the church been more lukewarm; and at no time has the individual believer been more pressured by worldliness. But the duty of Isaiah was plain—and so is ours.

With this in mind, we can see why Isaiah received such a vivid revelation of the Messiah. The Christ he saw was the Christ of the Bible, not the Christ that is commonly represented by present-day philosophers and liberal theologians.

CHRIST IN ISAIAH: PROPHECIES

The context in which Isaiah saw Christ is clearly defined in seven aspects of the book. We urge you to use them as a springboard for a more detailed study of the revelation of Jesus Christ in this marvelous Old Testament writing.

1. *Isaiah saw Christ in His preexistence.* The apostle John wrote, "These things said Isaiah, when he saw *His glory,* and spoke of Him" (John 12:41). A glorious and oft-quoted verse is Isaiah 9:6, "For unto us a child is born, unto us *a son is given,* and the government shall be upon His shoulder; and His name shall be called Wonderful, Counselor, The Mighty God, *The Everlasting Father,* The Prince of Peace." Isaiah saw Him and heard His name.

2. *Isaiah saw Christ in His incarnation* (Isaiah 7:14). You can't escape the necessity of the virgin birth. Who is this One born of a virgin? Immanuel, "God with us." "Therefore the Lord Himself shall give you a sign; behold, the virgin shall conceive, and bear a son, and shall call His name Immanuel" (7:14).

3. *Isaiah saw Christ in His suffering and death.* The 53rd chapter of Isaiah is inexhaustible in its presentation of the Lord Jesus. Each of the 12 verses finds literal fulfillment in Christ's rejection and crucifixion. Seven times we are told that He bore our sins. Isaiah saw the vicarious, substitutionary suffering of the Lord Jesus.

4. *Isaiah saw Christ in His resurrection.* The first clause of Isaiah 53:12 indicates this. "Therefore will I divide Him a portion with the great, and He shall divide the spoil with the strong...."

5. *Isaiah saw Christ in His intercession at the throne of God.* The last clause of verse 12 relates this wonderful truth. "He bore the sin of many, and made intercession for the transgressors."

6. *Isaiah saw Christ indwelling the believer through the Holy Spirit.* The first verse of Isaiah 55 transports you to the incident at Jacob's well in John 4, where Jesus identified Himself as the living water. "Ho, everyone that thirsteth, come to the waters, and he that hath no money; come, buy and eat; yea, come, buy wine and milk without money and without price" (Isaiah 55:1).

7. *Isaiah saw Christ in His second coming.* The 63rd chapter of this prophecy speaks of the tribulation that will occur at the close of this age. In chapter 11, and again in 65:19-25, Isaiah described the millennial reign of the Lord Jesus. The prophet even saw beyond the millennial reign, envisioning the new heaven and new earth in the eternal state.

Is it any wonder that when Philip joined the eunuch and found him reading Isaiah the prophet, Philip "began at the same scripture, and preached unto him Jesus" (Acts 8:35). Yes, Christ and His salvation figure prominently in the prophecy of Isaiah.

JEREMIAH

Jeremiah began his ministry about 60 years after the death of Isaiah. His name means, "whom the Lord sets or appoints." It might also mean, "elevated of the Lord." The word of the Lord came to Jeremiah when he was very young, during the 13th year of Josiah's reign. He prophesied during the reigns of Josiah, Jehoahaz, Jehoiakim, Jehoiachin, and Zedekiah. He was contemporary with Zephaniah, Habukkuk, Ezekiel, and Daniel. He delivered his discourse at irregular intervals during a period of more than 40 years. Therefore, no chronological order or logical arrangement can be given to the prophecy.

During Jeremiah's lifetime, Judah fell and was carried into captivity under Nebuchadnezzar. The Babylonian monarch beseiged and took Jerusalem. Jeremiah was first allowed to stay with the remnant in the land, but he was later taken with them to Egypt. We may presume that he died there.

Jeremiah is called the "weeping prophet," but he is also a prophet of hope. The key words of his prophecy are "go and cry..." (2:2).

OUTLINE OF THE BOOK
    I. Introduction (1)

As in the prophecy of Isaiah, the first chapter is a general introduction to the book. It tells of Jeremiah's call and his commissioning.

II. Complaints Against the Jews (2-20)

Jehovah's bitter complaints against the Jews for their perversity, idolatry, and manifold sins are publicized. The section ends with the tearful cry of the prophet's wounded heart. He even cursed the very day he was born.

III. Prophecies Against Individuals (21-29)

Jeremiah records specific predictions against individuals—Zedekiah, Shallum, Jehoiakim, and Coniah. False prophets and false priests are condemned. Included is the distinct announcement of the overthrow of the house of Judah by Nebuchadnezzar and the 70 years of Jewish captivity.

IV. Restoration of Israel (30-33)

The prophet looked forward to the promised restoration of Israel and their final reestablishment in their own land at the personal return of Jesus Christ.

V. Historical Narrative (34,35)

Events of the day are recorded that show the false confidence of princes and people, the contempt of the king for the Word of God, the imprisonment of Jeremiah, the capture and destruction of Jerusalem, and Jeremiah's release and removal to Egypt. The continuance of God's testimony is evident throughout.

VI. Judgments of Nations (46-49)

The condemnation of God upon seven Gentile nations surrounding Israel is presented.

VII. Doom of Babylon (50,51)

The fall of Babylon and the glorious redemption of Israel are prophesied. The section looks forward to a day of Jewish glory still to come.

VIII. Historical Appendix (52)

The conquest and captivity of Judah is reviewed.

CHRIST IN JEREMIAH

Many of the details of Jeremiah's activity depict the response of the nation of Israel to the first coming and the ministry of the Lord Jesus. You could write these words of the Lord Jesus over the pages of Jeremiah: "O Jerusalem, Jerusalem, thou that killest the prophets, and stonest them who are sent unto thee, how often would I have gathered thy children together, even as a hen gathereth her chickens under her wings, and ye would not!" (Matthew 23:37).

Let me direct your attention to some key points about the call and ministry of Jeremiah. Then we'll consider the similarities to the ministry of God's Servant, the Lord Jesus Christ.

1. *Jeremiah's call.* God had put His hand upon the prophet before he was born (1:4-9). The sovereign, omniscient, omnipotent God had called him. What a comfort this was to Jeremiah in the difficult years to follow! An illustration is found in the response of the people after he spoke at the temple. "Now it came to pass, when Jeremiah had ceased speaking all that the Lord had commanded him to speak unto all the people, that the priests and the prophets and all the people took him, saying, Thou shalt surely die" (26:8).

2. *Jeremiah's suffering.* Few men ever suffered for doing good as much as Jeremiah. He was imprisoned again and again. Chapter 20, verse 2, tells us that he was put in stocks. Chapter 38 records that he was lowered by ropes into a miry dungeon (probably a cistern), accused of treason, opposed by false prophets, and surrounded by his countrymen who were clamoring for his life. He was then carried away into Egypt and not permitted to die in his beloved Judah. We can readily see that his suffering at the hands of his own people is a type and picture of the agony of Christ.

3. *Jeremiah's message.* The words of Jehovah when He commissioned His servant are as follows: "For, behold, I have made thee this day a fortified city, and an iron pillar, and bronze walls against the whole land, against the kings of Judah, against its princes, against its priests, and against the people of the land" (1:18). That was a clean sweep! It took them all in—the throne, the politicians, the clergy, and the laity. His

126

message was against every Jew; consequently, it turned every Jew against him. Why did God ask this of His servant?

The nation was rushing headlong toward destruction. God thrust Jeremiah onto the scene to endeavor to save them. He was faced with a decision: should he go along with the crowd, or should he go with God?

To the east of Palestine were the mighty Assyrians, and Egypt was a strong threat on the south. So the frightened Jews were trying to play politics. God had said, "Go not down into Egypt for help" (42:19). Why did He give this command? Because *He alone* was their help. So Jeremiah sounded the message, "Repent! Repent! Repent!"

4. *An illustration.* If you want to know about the times of Jeremiah's work, look at chapter 36. The prophet is confined in prison, and his scribe Baruch is with him. God commanded Jeremiah to put into a scroll all the words that He had spoken against Israel, Judah, and the nations. Baruch transcribed this message. Did the people receive it? Jehudi, the king's servant, took the scroll, cut it with a knife, and cast it into the fire to destroy it. The record comments, "Yet they were not afraid, nor tore their garments, neither the king, nor any of his servants that heard all these words" (36:24).

Why did they refuse to listen? Because wicked people hate God's Word, for it testifies against their sins. The psalmist said, "But unto the wicked, God saith, What hast thou to do to declare My statutes, or that thou shouldest take My covenant in thy mouth, seeing thou hatest instruction, and castest My words behind thee?" (Psalm 50:16,17). Evil men seek to destroy God's Word because it tells of their doom.

But the wicked can no more destroy the written Word than they could the Living Word. "Forever, O Lord, Thy word is settled in heaven" (Psalm 119:89). Jesus spoke some very stringent words, recorded in John, when He asked the Jews, "If He called them gods, unto whom the word of God came, and the scripture cannot be broken, say ye of Him, whom the Father hath sanctified and sent into the world, Thou blasphemest; because I said, I am the Son of God?" (John 10:35,36). Jesus had earlier certified Jeremiah's words when He said, "Think not that I am come to destroy the law, or the prophets; I am not come to destroy, but to fulfill. For verily I say unto you, Till heaven and earth pass, one jot or one tittle shall in no way pass from the law, till all be fulfilled" (Matthew 5:17,18).

5. *A stabilizing hope.* You might think there is no bright side to the prophecy of Jeremiah, yet there is. God gave him a hopeful picture early in his ministry.

The word which came to Jeremiah from the Lord, saying,

Arise, and go down to the potter's house, and there I will cause thee to hear My words.

Then I went down to the potter's house, and, behold, he wrought a work on the wheels.

And the vessel that he made of clay was marred in the hand of the potter; so he made it again another vessel, as seemed good to the potter to make it (Jeremiah 18:1-4).

The story of the potter and his wheel, and the vessel the potter made again, describes what will happen to Israel in the future. The prophet also gave this promise:

Behold, the days come, saith the Lord, that I will raise unto David a righteous Branch, and a King shall reign and prosper, and shall execute justice and righteousness in the earth.

In His days Judah shall be saved, and Israel shall dwell safely; and this is His name whereby He shall be called, THE LORD OUR RIGHTEOUSNESS.

Therefore, behold, the days come, saith the Lord, that they shall no more say, The Lord liveth, who brought up the children of Israel out of the land of Egypt,

But, The Lord liveth, who brought up and who led the seed of the house of Israel out of the north country, and from all countries to which I had driven them, and they shall dwell in their own land (Jeremiah 23:5-8).

David Baron said, "You need not speculate upon Israel's history; it is written in a book." Then he reverently laid his hand upon chapters 30, 31, and 32 of the prophecy of Jeremiah. Peruse these chapters again, noting that Jehovah said "I will" at least 33 times in these three chapters. God is determined to reshape the "clay" and mold another vessel that will be pleasing to Himself. All of this work concerning the nation of Israel is still future, and it centers in the person of God's Son, Israel's Messiah, the Lord Jesus Christ. He is the One of whom the prophet spoke as follows:

Their Redeemer is strong, the Lord of hosts is His name; He shall thoroughly plead their cause, that He may give rest to the land, and disquiet the inhabitants of Babylon (Jeremiah 50:34).

LAMENTATIONS

Following the book of Jeremiah lies Lamentations, a poetic work by the "weeping prophet," which is full of instruction but is seldom read or preached. It is intricately composed. The first two chapters have 22 verses each and are an acrostic; that is, starting with *aleph*, the first word of each verse begins with the subsequent letter of the Hebrew alphabet. The third chapter of Lamentations has 66 verses, and each three-verse segment begins with a successive letter of the Hebrew alphabet. The fourth chapter is arranged like the first two. Chapter 5 also has 22 verses, but is not in acrostic arrangement. The structure of Lamentations is so amazing that the critics have said that Jeremiah could not have been the author, for he didn't have the ability it took to write it. Perhaps he didn't have the ability, but they ignore divine inspiration.

Lamentations is an unveiling of the great loving heart of Jehovah for His people. He chastens them, yet He loves them. God's sorrow and love are demonstrated through the heart expressions of Jeremiah.

If we were to choose a biblical text that captures the theme of the book, it would be either Proverbs 13:15, "... the way of transgressors is hard," or Romans 6:23,

"For the wages of sin is death." One writer has said, "Sin and salvation, like mighty rivers, flow right through the Bible and have come down through the ages together. With the one or the other every man is being borne along. The one floats on to the dead sea of eternal darkness, the other carries all who rest on its bosom into the ocean of God's infinite light and love." It is the first river, sin, that is seen in all its horror in the book of Lamentations.

This is the prophecy of weeping, the book of tears. The mood is set early in the first chapter when Jeremiah says of Jerusalem, "She weepeth bitterly in the night, and her tears are on her cheeks" (v. 2).

OUTLINE OF THE BOOK

    I. Tears for the City (1)
    II. Tears for the Daughter of Zion (2)
    III. Tears for the Man Who Has Seen Affliction (3)
    IV. Tears for the Precious Sons of Zion (4)
    V. Tears for the Orphans and Fatherless (5)

PRACTICAL TEACHING

Although the lamentations of Jeremiah are directed toward the people of Jerusalem, the great principles of the Bible expressing both God's hatred for sin and His desire to see the sinner repent are also in view.

The word "sin" literally means, "missing the mark." How graphically this is seen in the history of Israel, for no other nation has been so favored as that people! God delivered them by blood and by power from Egypt, brought them across the Red Sea on dry land, fed them for 40 years in the wilderness, and miraculously kept their clothes from wearing out and their sandals from becoming thin. With Joshua in command, they defeated the nations of Canaan. Their capital city, Jerusalem, was blessed of God. Their temple, and particularly the holy of holies, became the dwelling place of God.

The glory of God filled the place. Although this is how Lamentations begins: "How doth the city sit lonely, that was full of people; how is she become a widow! She that was great among the nations, a princess among the provinces; how is she become a vassal!" (1:1). Why was this? The people had "missed the mark." God had asked them to follow Him and to keep His statutes, so that other nations might have the knowledge of the one true God. But Israel had failed and now was suffering the fruit of her sin.

Sin and its results cannot be disassociated; labor that is rendered must receive proper payment. If something is earned, it is unjust to hold back the wages. The condemned sinner can never accuse God of injustice. In Lamentations 1:18 the principle is stated: "The Lord is righteous; for I have rebelled against His commandment."

This law is immutable; it will never be changed. Chapter 2 of Lamentations makes no mention of Nebuchadnezzar nor the armies of Babylon. Why? Because Israel realized that the law of God was at work. The New Testament states it this way: "Whatever a man soweth, that shall he also reap" (Galatians 6:7).

You will find it an interesting study to count the number of times the words "He hath" are used in chapter 2. God was executing His righteousness by paying the people of Israel the wages they had earned because of their sin.

Lamentations 3 presents another consequence of sin, the suffering of the innocent. Though the prophet delivered God's truth, he was hated, hunted, and hounded. He suffered the most. The greater the innocence, the greater the suffering.

CHRIST IN LAMENTATIONS

We can see a picture of the Lord Jesus in the suffering of Jeremiah, and the people who rejected and persecuted the prophet portray the religious leaders of Israel who rejected their Messiah. In your mind's eye, move some 600 years from Jeremiah's day into the future. If the feelings of Jeremiah as expressed in chapter 3 are feelings common to every man, then what must have been the feelings of the Son of God! Read again Christ's words of lament for Jerusalem.

O Jerusalem, Jerusalem, thou that killest the prophets, and stonest them who are sent unto thee, how often would I have gathered thy children together, even as a hen gathereth her chickens under her wings, and ye would not!

Behold, your house is left unto you desolate.

For I say unto you, Ye shall not see Me henceforth, till ye shall say, Blessed is He that cometh in the name of the Lord (Matthew 23:37-39).

The Lord Jesus expressed the intensity of His suffering in the words spoken in Gethsemane. They serve to reinforce the fact that His holy nature must have recoiled at the thought of bearing the sins of the world and of dying at the hands of God's chosen race.

As you observe the name "Lord" used in Lamentations, remember that this is the name "Jehovah." This name designates the covenant-keeping God, the God of redemption, and therefore is a reflection of the Lord Jesus Christ.

THE CLOSING CHAPTER

Chapter 5 of Lamentations is a prayer. It is a prayer of confession (vv. 1,7,16), and it is a prayer of hope (v. 19). Note what that hope is founded upon: the eternal, never-changing God, the Redeemer. Then too, it is a prayer for future blessing (v. 21).

We are reminded of that dark day pictured in John 6. Our Lord had begun to speak of His death and had indicated that the only approach to God the Father was through Him. At the mention of His impending death, the crowds that had followed Him for the loaves and the fish "went back, and walked no more with Him" (v. 66). To the handful of disciples that remained, the Lord Jesus posed this searching question: "Will ye also go away?" (v. 67). The response of Simon Peter was filled with the language of faith as he replied, "Lord, to whom shall we go? Thou hast the words of eternal life. And we believe and are sure that Thou art that Christ, the Son of the living God" (John 6:68,69).

In Jeremiah's day, the prospects were bleak for Jerusalem and the nation of Israel, and the prophet mourned the predicted judgment upon their sin. Even so, he knew that restoration, return, and blessing could be found only in Jehovah, the Redeemer. Likewise, the sinner, no matter how deeply he may have transgressed, how vile his past, how extensive his iniquity, can find cleansing, new life, and future hope in one person—Jesus Christ. The Jehovah of the Old Testament is the Lord Jesus of the New. The tears of sorrow and suffering are wiped away by the One who cleanses and forgives all who come in faith to Him.

EZEKIEL

During the time between the surrender of Jerusalem by the worthless King Jehoiachin and its destruction under Zedekiah, many of the nobles of Judah were taken as captives to Babylon. The prophet Jeremiah remained in the city until its overthrow. He sent a message to the captives, recorded in the 29th chapter of his prophecy, warning them against the delusion of believing that they would soon return from their exile. Among those captives was a young man by the name of Ezekiel, a member of the priestly line who also became a prophet. His name means "God shall strengthen" or "strength of God." Like Jeremiah, his prophecy was principally concerned with Judah and Jerusalem, though it did extend to "the house of Israel."

A new generation had been born during the exile, and Ezekiel brought to them a testimony of the judgment that would fall upon their beloved city. He also presented the reason for that judgment.

Like Isaiah before him, Ezekiel was granted a vision of God. Isaiah's experience focused upon the holiness of God; Ezekiel's centered not only upon holiness but also upon God's glory.

Except for Revelation, no book in the divine library contains so many symbols. Ezekiel said that while he was a captive by the river Chebar, "... the heavens were opened, and I saw visions of God" (1:1).

OUTLINE OF THE BOOK

I. Ezekiel's Vision and Commission (1-3)

This records the prophet's initial vision of the cherubim and the glory of God, and his commission as a watchman over Israel.

II. Visions of Judgment (4-11)

The prophet receives a series of strange signs and visions that reveal the wickedness of the people and the coming judgment. The glory of God is seen departing from the temple.

III. Visions of Captivity (12-24)

Ezekiel is transported in the Spirit to Babylon, where he receives further signs and visions of reproof and impending doom. He gives news of the homeland to the exiles.

IV. Judgment on Gentile Nations (25-32)

The sentence of judgment is pronounced upon seven Gentile powers.

V. Desolation and Restoration Prophesied (33-37)

Ezekiel hears of Jerusalem's fall. A long desolation upon Palestine is predicted, and the literal restoration of Israel is promised at the return of Christ, the true Shepherd.

VI. Invasion from the North (38,39)

After the restoration, a northern confederation headed by Russia will camp in the mountains of Judea and be destroyed by the Lord.

VII. Glory Returns to Israel (40-48)

With the enemies of Israel crushed and the nation spiritually reborn, the glory of God returns. The temple is rebuilt, and God's anointed Ruler is worshiped as king over all the earth. The holy city is named Jehovah-Shammah, "The Lord is there" (48:35).

We will now consider several of the key passages of Ezekiel, centering our attention upon the reflections of Christ that occur throughout the book.

EZEKIEL'S COMMISSION (chapter 1)

In vision, the prophet saw the cherubim, who "had the likeness of a man" (v. 5). Each had four faces: the face of a lion, an ox, a man, and an eagle. Wherever cherubim are mentioned in the Bible, they are either guarding or declaring the holiness of God. And where but in the person of the Lord Jesus Christ is the holiness of God more fully displayed and declared? He is *the lion,* the King who has the right to reign. Like the beast of servitude, *the ox,* He is the Servant of Jehovah. He said that He did not come to be ministered to, but to serve, and to "give His life a ransom for many" (Matthew 20:28). He is the Word made flesh, dwelling among us (John 1:14). He is therefore the perfect *man.* Beyond that, He soars higher than any other, and like the *eagle,* He can look directly into the face of God with unblinking eye. This is because He is more than perfect man; He is God manifest in the flesh. "In the beginning was the Word, and the Word was with God, and the Word was God" (John 1:1).

Ezekiel's vision of the Lord prepared him for his ministry. Throughout the book this phrase appears repeatedly: "The word of the Lord came unto me." This was his authority, and its recurrence may form the divisions of the book. Another phrase that occurs frequently is: "They shall know that I am Jehovah."

GOD'S DECREE (21:27)

The Lord pronounced these solemn words recorded in Ezekiel:

> I will overturn, overturn, overturn it, and it shall be no more, until He comes whose right it is; and I will give it Him (21:27).

This prophecy was uttered 600 years before Christ came. It is preceded by these awesome words of God: "Remove the diadem, and take off the crown" (v. 26). From the deliverance of this prophecy until now, the world has gone through a process of overturning, of the removing of diadems, and of kingdoms falling. Jerusalem, the crossroads of the world, has been at the center of anarchy, change, confusion, and misrule. What has been true of Jerusalem has also been true of the whole world. Not a government in all the world has the slightest assurance that it will remain for many more years. The "overturning" has entered every realm of life—not only the political but the ecclesiastical, the social, and the economic as well. Yes, world conditions today paint a dark picture indeed! Even so, a few Bible scholars are teaching that through the good offices of the church a spiritual millennium is coming. Never!

THE REIGN OF THE RIGHTFUL KING

The "overturning" will continue until the coming of the One "whose right it is" to reign (21:27). And who is that? Jesus Christ, God's appointed Ruler. He is the anointed One, earth's Redeemer and Israel's Messiah. The promise of God the Father is, "... and I will give it Him" (v. 27). This is what the world needs today. Until the Prince of Peace comes, the governments of this earth will be characterized by instability and unrest.

With this truth in his heart, and with the stability of the throne of God before his eyes, Ezekiel was ready for an unfolding of the future. He saw it as few have ever been permitted to see it.

Ezekiel 37 records a great vision. The Spirit of God put the prophet in a valley that was full of dry bones. There came a great shaking, and the bones began to come together. Flesh and skin then appeared upon them, but no life was in them. Ezekiel watched as, at the command of the Lord God, breath came into the assembled bodies from the four winds, and they came to life. They rose to their feet as a great army of men.

God Himself interpreted the vision for Ezekiel. He identified the bones as "the whole house of Israel" (37:11). He then told Ezekiel to say on His behalf,

Behold, O My people, I will open your graves, and cause you to come up out of your graves, and bring you into the land of Israel.

And ye shall know that I am the Lord, when I have opened your graves, O My people, and brought you up out of your graves,

And shall put My Spirit in you, and ye shall live, and I shall place you in your own land; then shall ye know that I, the Lord, have spoken it, and performed it, saith the Lord (Ezekiel 37:12-14).

God gave further information to the listening prophet in verse 22. "And I will make them one nation in the land upon the mountains of Israel, and one king shall be king to them all." The kingdom will be united in the endtime. Chapter 37 closes with this promise of Jehovah: "And the nations shall know that I, the Lord, do sanctify Israel, when My sanctuary shall be in the midst of them forevermore" (v. 28). Who is this One in the midst of restored and resurrected Israel? It is none other than Jehovah, the Lord Jesus Christ.

Chapters 40 through 48 describe a scene never before witnessed upon this earth. What is it? The magnificent millennial temple.

The prophecy of Ezekiel closes with the presence of the Lord (the Lord Jesus Christ) reigning and ruling in Jerusalem. ". . . and the name of the city from that day shall be, The Lord is there" (48:35).

DANIEL

The prophecy of Daniel is one of the most important books in the entire Word of God. It introduces us to the realm of New Testament prophecy. Like Ezekiel, the author was a child of the captivity, and both prophets were contemporaries of Jeremiah. The Holy Spirit commissioned Daniel during the Babylonian captivity for a specific purpose. His inspired testimony would open "the times of the Gentiles," an important new era in God's redemptive plan. In fact, from verse 4 of chapter 2 to the close of chapter 7, the original writing was not in Hebrew but in Chaldean, the language of Babylon. It's almost as if God were saying to the kingdoms of the world, "Read in your own language what shall be the end of your boasted power."

The book of Daniel marks out the exact course the nations of the world will take. It tells how the kingdoms of this earth shall become the kingdom of our Lord and His Christ (see Revelation 11:15). If the Jews had been receptive, I believe they could have calculated from Daniel the exact day their Messiah would present Himself. And the Savior referred to this book when He spoke of the signs of His return to earth.

The book of Daniel has two major divisions: Historical, chapters 1 through 6; Prophetical, chapters 7 through 12. However, even the historical segments contain prophecy, for the characteristic features of Gentile dominion are exhibited in the narratives that provide the background for Daniel's visions.

OUTLINE OF THE BOOK

I. Introduction (1)

The personal history of Daniel and his faithfulness to God is recorded here.

II. The Vision of Nebucnadnezzar (2,3)

    A. The forgotten dream and failure of the wise men of Babylon to interpret it (2:1-12).

    B. The revelation of the king's dream to Daniel (2:13-26).

    C. The vision presented with the interpretation (2:27-45). *The head of gold* represents Babylon, Nebuchadnezzar, and his monarchy. This is the beginning of the "times of the Gentiles" (Luke 21:24). *The breasts and arms of silver* represent Medo-Persia, the kingdom that followed Nebuchadnezzar and was inferior to it. *The belly and thighs of brass* represent Greece under Alexander the Great. *The legs of iron* are Rome, divided in two (Eastern and Western). *The toes,* part of iron and part of clay, represent a deterioration. The Stone "cut out of the mountain without hands" depicts Jesus Christ and His glorious appearing (v. 45). His return will spell the destruction of Gentile dominion, and He will be exalted to world rulership.

    D. The pride of Nebuchadnezzar (2:46-3:30).

III. The Tree Vision (4)

Daniel said to Nebuchadnezzar, "The tree that thou sawest . . . it is thou, O king" (vv. 20-22). That tree was to be cut down. The proud king of Babylon was made to eat grass like an ox until he recognized that God the

Most High rules in the kingdoms of the world and gives them to whomever He will.

IV. The Pride of Belshazzar (5)

Belshazzar and a thousand of his lords, while engaged in a licentious drinking feast, desecrated the sacred vessels of the Jewish temple. Handwriting suddenly appeared on the wall, and Daniel was brought in to interpret it. The predicted event, the fall of Belshazzar, signaled the end of the first world Gentile rule and the beginning of the second under Darius the Mede.

V. From Darius to Cyrus (6)

Daniel defied the king's decree that prohibited asking a petition of any god or man except the king for 30 days. Anyone who violated this rule would be cast into the den of lions. Daniel remained faithful to his God and prayed three times a day as he always had, with his windows opened toward Jerusalem. Consequently, he was cast into the den of lions, but the Lord delivered him by shutting the mouths of the lions.

VI. The Vision of the Four Beasts (7)

The difference between this vision and Nebuchadnezzar's similar vision (chapter 2) is that the king was seeing from the standpoint of man, while Daniel saw from the viewpoint of God. The great image of chapter 2 presents the outward appearance of Gentile domination, while the beast vision of chapter 4 depicts the true character of Gentile rule as ravenous, cruel, and selfish. The national symbol of many world powers today is of a beast or bird of prey.

The great sea in Scripture is usually a symbol of the mass of humanity. Out of the "great sea" came these four beasts:

    A. The lion, representing Nebuchadnezzar and Babylon (v. 4).

    B. The lopsided bear, symbolizing Medo-Persia (v. 5).

    C. The leopard, speaking of the Grecian power of Alexander, later divided into four heads after his death (v. 6).

    D. The nondescript beast representing Roman

world power. The 10 horns are "ten kings that shall arise" (v. 7).

E. The "little horn" depicts an eleventh king who will rise up among the 10 and overcome 3 of them (read 2 Thessalonians 2:1-10; Revelation 13:1-8).

F. The "Ancient of days" appears (vv. 21-27).

VII. The Ram and Rough Goat Vision (8)

The interpretation is given in verses 21-25. The ram with two horns is Medo-Persia, and the rough goat is Alexander the Great. The "little horn" of this vision is a forerunner or example of the "little horn" of chapter 7. Antiochus Epiphanes, the "little horn" of this 8th chapter, entered the temple and sacrificed a pig on the altar. This was the first "abomination of desolation of the holy place."

VIII. The Vision of the Seventy Weeks (9)

Sir Edward Denny, English theologian of the last century, said, "This is the backbone of prophecy." The 70 weeks are divided into units of 7, 62, and 1. "Week" used here is a generic term like "dozen" or "score," and in this Scripture it indicates a 7-year timespan (a week of years). Let's look at the divisions of this important prophecy:

A. *Seven Weeks.* In 49 years, the city of Jerusalem would be rebuilt. This was fulfilled in the time of Ezra and Nehemiah.

B. *Sixty-two Weeks.* The Messiah, the Prince, would be "cut off" 434 years (62x7) after the rebuilding of Jerusalem. This was fulfilled when Christ was crucified. Sir Robert Anderson and Royal Astronomer G. B. Airy have calculated that the timespan from the day the order was issued in Nehemiah 2:1 for the rebuilding of Jerusalem (445 B.C.) until the day of Christ's triumphal entry (A.D. 32) was exactly 173,880 days. This figure is the result of multiplying 483 prophetic years (Daniel's 69 "weeks") by 360 days. That this is the current timespan for a prophetic year seems to be clearly indicated in the book of Revelation where the 3 1/2 years or 42 months of the Great Tribulation is designated as 1260 days (11:2; 12:6; 12:14; 13:5). After the 483 years were over, Messiah was cut off. The prophetic clock stopped. God's dealings today do not center upon Israel; rather, He is taking out of the Gentiles "a people for His name" (Acts 15:14).

C. *One week.* Seven years of the prophecy remain to be fulfilled (v. 27). Antichrist, the "little horn" of chapter 7, will make a covenant with the Jews, then he will break that covenant in the middle of this "week" of years. We believe that this 70th week is the great tribulation period spoken of by our Lord in Matthew 24:15-28. This is the "time of trouble" prophesied in Daniel 12:1 and the "hour of temptation" mentioned by the risen Christ in Revelation 3.

IX. The Vision of Glory (10)

This vision was given to the prophet in the third year of the reign of King Cyrus. It was designed to make Daniel understand what would happen to his people, the Jews, in the latter days. "For yet the vision is for many days" (v. 14).

X. Concluding Prophetic Visions (11,12)
  A. Three more kings of Medo-Persia (11:1,2).
  B. The division and rule of Alexander's empire (11:3-20).
  C. The "little horn" of chapter 8 is Antiochus Epiphanes (11:21-35).
  D. The "little horn" of chapter 7 is Antichrist (11:36-45).
  E. The great tribulation (12:1).
  F. The resurrection and God's final message to Daniel (12:2-13).

CHRIST IN THE BOOK OF DANIEL

We cannot consider the prophetic Scriptures without coming eventually to the One who is the Spirit of prophecy, the Lord Jesus Christ. He is the Smiting Stone of Daniel 2. God's Son is the One who shall come to destroy Gentile dominion. It is He whose kingdom "shall stand forever."

Nebuchadnezzar looked into the fiery furnace and

said, "Lo, I see four men loose, walking in the midst of the fire, and they have no hurt; and the form of the fourth is like a son of the gods" (Daniel 3:25). He did not know of whom he spoke, but this no doubt was a theophany, a pre-incarnate appearance of the Lord Jesus.

What a majestic scene in chapter 7! The Ancient of days, God the Father, is seated upon His throne. The time setting is immediately before the return of Christ to establish His kingdom. We read, "I saw in the night visions, and, behold, one like the Son of man came with the clouds of heaven, and came to the Ancient of days . . ." (v. 13). The verses that follow are paralleled by the description of Christ in Revelation 5:1-7. "And there was given Him dominion, and glory, and a kingdom, that all people, nations, and languages should serve Him; His dominion is an everlasting dominion, which shall not pass away, and His kingdom that which shall not be destroyed" (Daniel 7:14,15).

Daniel 9 foretells the death of Messiah, the Prince.

Like a thread of gold, the assurance of the ultimate triumph of our Lord runs through the prophecy of Daniel. Indeed, He is Lord of lords, and King of kings.

The Lord Jesus Himself quoted from this book of Daniel (Matthew 24:14,15,30; Luke 21:24; Matthew 26:63,64). He used the prophecy of Daniel about the coming of the Son of man in clouds of heaven as proof of His messiahship and deity.

HOSEA

Hosea is the first and the longest of the group of books we call "the minor prophets." He was a contemporary of Amos in Israel and of Isaiah and Micah in Judah. He prophesied in Judah during and following the Assyrian captivity of the Northern Kingdom—an era in which the Southern Kingdom was both greatly prosperous and very corrupt. The name "Hosea" means "deliverance" or "salvation." He lived during the long and vigorous reign of Jeroboam II, king of Israel. Unlike the prophet Isaiah, who was burdened chiefly about Judah and Jerusalem, Hosea was principally occupied in expressing the sorrow of Jehovah for the Northern Kingdom. The children of Israel had broken His covenant and hardened their hearts against Him.

Hosea became a part of his own message. The prophet had an unfaithful wife, Gomer. In spite of her persistent sin and shameful life, Hosea continued to cherish her. After her lovers had abandoned her, Hosea found her in the slave market, paid the price to reclaim her, forgave her, and took her again as his wife. By enduring this grief, his heart was prepared to deliver the message of Jehovah to Israel, the nation that had been unfaithful to the Lord and had committed spiritual adultery.

OUTLINE OF THE BOOK

   I. The Moral State of Israel (1-3)
  II. The Sins of God's People (4-13:13)
 III. The Conversion and Blessing of Israel
      (13:14-14)

Let us now consider each of these sections carefully.

Chapters 1 through 3 depict the moral condition of Israel. The nation had been a wife to Jehovah. He had committed to her the honor of His name, but she had become an adulteress (1:2,3). The names given to the prophet's children tell us a number of things about the effect of Israel's sin.

"Jezreel" (1:4,5). This is a reminder that God had not condoned the sin of Jehu (2 Kings 10:1-14), nor had He forgotten all the crimes of Israel.

"Lo-ruhamah" (1:6). The word means "unpitied," signifying that Jehovah's mercy would not continue indefinitely but that judgment would soon come.

"Lo-ammi" (1:8,9). This name means "not my people" and showed that Israel would cease to be God's peculiar people. This was never said of Judah.

Then Jehovah promised to restore both Israel and Judah—a prophecy that remains to be fulfilled in the future (1:10,11). They will one day be reunited and reestablished as the earthly representative of Jehovah (see Romans 9:25,26).

Chapter 2 reveals both God's grief at Israel's sin and His unchanging love as demonstrated in His willingness to take her back. Verse 23 of chapter 2 is interpreted in Romans 9:26 as referring to the conversion of the Gentiles.

Next the wife of Hosea is brought back (3:1-3). Then follows a prediction that is being literally fulfilled today: "For the children of Israel shall abide many days without a king, and without a prince, and without a sacrifice, and without an image, and without an ephod, and without teraphim" (3:4). The prophecy of verse 5 will also be literally fulfilled: "Afterward shall the children of Israel return, and seek the Lord, their

God, and David, their king, and shall fear the Lord and His goodness in the latter days."

The specific sins of God's people are enumerated in Part II of Hosea (4-13:13). The Lord said, "My people are destroyed for lack of knowledge" (4:6). He went on to explain that the knowledge lacking in Israel was not financial, scientific, or commercial; but "thou hast forgotten the law of thy God" (v. 6). Jehovah spoke with bold, blunt words, signifying that the Israelites had insulted His holiness and outraged His love. He delivered a heavy indictment against Israel.

The final section of the prophecy depicts the future conversion and blessing of Israel (13-14:14). It begins with the prediction of coming judgment, which was fulfilled when Israel was carried away to Assyria. Judah continued to survive for more than a century and a half, but then she fell. A remnant of Judah returned to Palestine, but Israel did not. The book closes with a description of the day that is coming when Israel and Judah, at the verge of destruction because of iniquity, will return unto the Lord and experience His healing (14:4-9).

PRACTICAL TEACHING OF HOSEA

A number of useful lessons may be learned from a study of this book.

1. Worldliness in God's people, whenever it occurs, is designated by God with the word of Hosea 1:2 as "harlotry." In his epistle, James calls it spiritual "adultery" (James 4:4).

2. God's Word is always revealing. "Hear the word of the Lord" is Hosea's constant plea. The psalmist said, "Wherewithal shall a young man cleanse his way? By taking heed thereto according to Thy word" (Psalm 119:9).

3. Israel's failure is a picture of the church's sin. The church has forgotten that she is espoused to God, and her committing of spiritual adultery is evident in many realms.

4. The heartcry of God for the backslider and spir-

itual adulterer is expressed in the words, "How shall I give thee up, Ephraim?" (11:8).

5. A final view of God's mercy to the repentant and returning one is found in His promise: "I will be as the dew unto Israel" (14:5). Truly, God's mercy endures forever.

CHRIST IN HOSEA

The apostle Peter and the apostle Paul both alluded to Hosea 1:10 as having to do with the Messiah (1 Peter 2:10; Romans 9:25,26).

Israel's rejection of their King—their true "High Priest after the order of Melchizedek"—and the sacrifice which He offered has brought the people into the place where they have neither king nor prince nor sacrifice (Hosea 3:4). The verse that follows describes their glorious future, which is made possible because the people will seek the Lord their God and their Messiah, the Lord Jesus Christ (v. 5).

Resurrection is spoken of in Hosea 6:2. Whenever the "third day" is mentioned in the Scriptures, look carefully and you will see some connection with the resurrection of Christ. In a very real sense, not only is our resurrection made possible because of His, but the resurrection of the nation of Israel also depends upon the crucified, buried, and risen Christ.

Hosea also recorded these words of Jehovah: "I . . . called My Son out of Egypt" (11:1). This prophecy had its primary fulfillment in Israel's 400-year sojourn. But we learn from Matthew 2:15 that the real fulfillment of Hosea's prophecy is in the Lord Jesus Christ, the Son of God.

Near the end of Hosea's prophecy, Jehovah, the covenant-keeping Redeemer, said, ". . . there is no savior beside Me" (13:4). Of course, the Jehovah of the Old Testament is the Lord Jesus Christ of the New. "Neither is there salvation in any other; for there is no other name under heaven given among men, whereby we must be saved" (Acts 4:12). An angel of the Lord appeared unto Joseph and assured him that he did not need to fear taking Mary to be his wife, "for that which is conceived in her is of the Holy Spirit" (Matthew 1:20). The angel also said, "Thou shalt call His name Jesus; for He shall save His people from their sins" (Matthew 1:21). Hosea stated a great truth, which the apostle Paul affirmed when he wrote, "For there is one God, and one mediator between God and men, the man, Christ Jesus, who gave Himself a ransom for all, to be testified in due time" (1 Timothy 2:5,6).

JOEL

Although the book of Joel contains only three chapters
and is seldom read, it is one of the most stirring of all
the prophetic writings. The date of the book is uncer-
tain because it names no kings. However, many feel
that Joel must have prophesied during the reign of
Joash (2 Chronicles 22-24). If so, he was a contemporary of Elisha. His name means, "Jehovah is God," and
he prophesied to a people who had forgotten that.

This prophecy surveys the history of Israel from the
time it was given to the second advent of Christ. The
book is an illustration of how God makes the future
known to man; in fact, it illustrates the way all biblical
truth is revealed. It demonstrates that revelation is
progressive. Joel unfolds and develops a new concept,
the day of the Lord, as do the prophets that follow him.
The three aspects of his vision increase in scope as the
book progresses.

OUTLINE OF THE BOOK
    I. A Plague Destroys the Land (1:1-5)
    II. The Vision of the Invading Army (1:6-2:27)
    III. Future Judgment and Deliverance (2:28-3:21)

Every book of the Bible has its own key to its interpretation. Sometimes the key is at the front door of the book; other times at the back door. The key to the prophecy of Joel is found near the front door: "Alas for the day! For the day of the Lord is at hand, and as a destruction from the Almighty shall it come" (Joel 1:15).

The land of Palestine had been a wonderful place. The hills were dotted with fig and olive trees, the slopes were covered with luxuriant vineyards, and the valleys were filled with corn. It had previously been described in metaphor as "a land that floweth with milk and honey" (Joshua 5:6). But when Joel was called to prophesy, a terrible judgment had befallen it.

THE LOCUST JUDGMENT

Four plagues had come upon the land: palmer worms, locusts, canker worms, and caterpillars. Some of the best authorities on the locust, as well as Hebrew scholars, maintain that four stages of the development of the locust are described here. The context shows what they did to their fair land. The advance column destroyed every leaf and blade of grass. Those that followed even devoured the bark from the trees. The noise of their wings was heard for miles, and the land looked as though it had been swept by fire.

The prophet revealed the cause for the plagues. These scourges had come from God as chastisement upon the people because of their sin. Although the judgment was regional in nature, it was filled with prophetic importance.

INVASION BY ASSYRIA PROPHESIED

The Lord said through Joel, "For a nation is come up upon My land, strong, and without number, whose teeth are the teeth of a lion, and he hath the cheek teeth of a great lion" (1:6). The specific prediction of invasion is recorded in chapter 2. The primary reference is to the impending invasion by Assyria, but the fuller picture is of the day of the Lord. The Assyrian invasion was but a shadow of something far more terrible to come. The devastation by the invading Assyrians fulfills the prophecy, but a complete and greater fulfillment will occur in the day of the Lord. In chapters 2 and 3, Joel spans the centuries and gives to us by inspiration a detailed description of the time that will close this age and usher in the next.

The armies will surround Jerusalem. As the locusts had attacked and destroyed the land, and as the nations of Babylon and Assyria would attack and destroy, so the endtime will be characterized by warfare and destruction. Compare Joel 2:1-10 with Zechariah 14:1 and 3, where the prophet warned, "Behold, the day of the Lord cometh, and thy spoil shall be divided in the midst of thee. For I will gather all nations against Jerusalem to battle; and the city shall be taken, and the houses rifled, and the women ravished; and half of the city shall go forth into captivity, and the residue of the people shall not be cut off from the city." This is in keeping with our Lord's dire prediction in the Olivet Discourse, "Verily I say unto you, There shall not be left here one stone upon another, that shall not be thrown down . . . . And except those days should be shortened, there should no flesh be saved; but for the elect's sake those days shall be shortened" (Matthew 24:2,22).

Joel 2:11 declares that the Lord's "army" (the locusts) is already in the land. Men have always failed to take Jehovah into account. Read again the story of Sennacherib and the Assyrians, and recall how God intervened to destroy that army. All of this is a picture of what will happen in the future. Joel declared the intent of Jehovah when he wrote, "I will also gather all nations, and will bring them down into the Valley of Jehoshaphat, and will judge them there for My people and for My heritage, Israel . . ." (Joel 3:2). This is what John saw in Revelation 19:17-19, and is preceded by the regathering of Judah to Jerusalem (Joel 3:11).

THE OUTPOURING OF THE SPIRIT

A plan is revealed in Joel 2:28-32. Note the words, "And it shall come to pass *afterward* . . . ." When Peter quoted this passage on the day of Pentecost, he did not say that the scene they witnessed was the fulfillment of the prophecy, but simply that "this is that which was spoken through the prophet, Joel" (Acts 2:16). We know that many of the signs accompanying the prediction were not witnessed on the day of Pentecost. There was no blood or fire or vaporous smoke. The sun was not turned into darkness, nor the moon into blood. These signs did not follow the coming of the Spirit in Peter's day because Israel was not repentant and obedient. But they will appear just before the glorious return of Christ. They will surely be seen in that future day.

THE DAY OF THE LORD

Chapter 3 of Joel's prophecy gives us the order of events for that period of time known as "the day of the Lord." We list them briefly with accompanying Scriptures for you to study.

1. The regathering of Judah to Jerusalem (v. 1). Compare Zechariah 10:6.

2. The gathering of the Gentile powers against Jerusalem (vv. 3, 9-15). Compare Revelation 17:12-15; Revelation 19:17-19.

3. God's controversy with the Gentile powers over their treatment of His people (vv. 2-8). Consult Deuteronomy 30:5-7; Matthew 25:31-45.

4. The Deliverer who came out of Zion (vv. 15,16). See Joel 2:32. In connection with this tremendous event, the reader will do well to study Obadiah, Romans 11:26-29, and Revelation 19:11-21.

5. The millennial blessing of Israel with Jehovah dwelling in Zion (Joel 3:17-21). This will be the time of ingathering, the time of Jewish conversion. Isaiah spoke of that time as follows: "And it shall come to pass in the last days, that the mountain of the Lord's house shall be established in the top of the mountains, and shall be exalted above the hills; and all nations shall flow unto it. And many people shall go and say, Come ye, and let us go up to the mountain of the Lord, to the house of the God of Jacob; and He will teach us of His ways, and we will walk in His paths; for out of Zion

shall go forth the law, and the word of the Lord from Jerusalem" (Isaiah 2:2,3).

Joel sets forth the mighty works of Jehovah, our Lord Jesus Christ, both in judgment and blessing upon His covenant people Israel. He "shall roar out of Zion, and utter His voice from Jerusalem, and the heavens and the earth shall shake; but the Lord will be the hope of His people, and the strength of the children of Israel" (Joel 3:16).

AMOS

During the time of great spiritual decline in Israel, God chose Elijah, an obscure man from the mountains of Gilead, and used him to turn the nation from its idolatry. One hundred fifty years later, Jeroboam II was on the throne. Great prosperity was in Israel, but also great wickedness prevailed. So God put His hand upon another man of the outdoors, Amos. He was a herdsman of Tekoa, a village located 5 miles south of Bethlehem. Although he lived in the Southern Kingdom, he prophesied primarily to the Northern Kingdom.

This is what he said of himself, "I am no prophet, neither am I a prophet's son, but I am an herdsman, and a gatherer of sycamore fruit; and the Lord took me as I followed the flock, and the Lord said unto me, Go, prophesy unto My people, Israel" (Amos 7:14,15). Amos had a double-faceted message from God: first, he denounced the sins of Israel; second, Amos looked beyond the sin and judgment and saw the triumph to follow. God will not let sin thwart His purposes.

A striking verse of this prophecy sets the theme: "And the Lord said unto me, Amos, what seest thou? And I said, A plumb line. Then said the Lord, Behold, I will set a plumb line in the midst of My people, Israel" (Amos 7:8). God does not overlook sin.

OUTLINE OF THE BOOK

I. Predictions of Judgment on Surrounding Peoples (1:1-2:3)

II. Predictions of Judgment upon Jerusalem and Judah (2:4-16)

III. The Sentence of Judgment against the "House of Jacob" (3:1-9:7)

Although Israel, the 10-tribe kingdom, is particularly in view, this foretelling takes in the whole family of Israel. Amos exposes the moral corruption and the apostasy of the people.

IV. Promise of Restoration and Glory (9:8-15)

The house of Jacob would be preserved, the throne of David restored, and glory given to the kingdom. This will be fulfilled at the second coming of Christ.

AMOS' MESSAGE AGAINST SIN (6:1-8)

Perhaps the greatest reason for the prophet's condemnation of Israel was that the people were "at ease." They were indolent, sinful, and indifferent to the Lord. All of this was at a time when great unrighteousness marked the nation. It will help if we consider what characterized this unrighteousness.

1. *A dependence upon natural things* (v. 1). In effect, the people of Israel said, "Look at our fortifications; these very mountains are our bulwarks." How often this is the attitude of God's heavenly people today, the church! We boast about our buildings, our great expenditures of money, our large staff, our growing prestige. But God says, "Not by might, nor by power, but by My Spirit" (Zechariah 4:6). God's work is not dependent upon our natural resources. The apostle Paul declared, "And base things of the world, and things which are despised, hath God chosen, yea, and things which are not, to bring to nothing things that are, that no flesh should glory in His presence" (1 Corinthians 1:28,29).

2. *A false optimism* (v. 3). The prophets would often draw attention to coming calamities. But the people

would say, "The evil day is far off; it will not come in our generation." The attitude today parallels that of Amos' time. We are slow to accept what the Scripture explicitly declares—that perilous days are ahead, that a religion will arise without power, that a departure from the faith will occur, and that Christians will reject sound doctrine. Yes, a false optimism prevails today in spite of the clear teaching of the Word of God.

3. *They lived in luxury* (v. 4). The people were self-sufficient and had forgotten their need for God. High living characterized the lifestyle of Israel. And Jesus observed during His earthly ministry, "So is he that layeth up treasure for himself, and is not rich toward God" (Luke 12:21).

4. *They were absorbed in the culture of music* (v. 5). "That chant to the sound of the harp, and invent to themselves instruments of music." What a marvelous gift music is! But sin has spoiled it, and the curse is clearly evident in that realm of human activity. All creation was once in tune in the major mode. The morning stars sang together. One day this major mode will return, and the trees will burst forth in music. But Israel's music appealed to the flesh; it was sensual. The people said in so many words, "Our music must be all right; it is just like David's."

A SURVEY OF THE BOOK

The Holy Spirit through the prophet Amos announced a series of judgments upon seven nations (chapters 1,2). This was followed by three searching messages to Israel, each beginning with the phrase, "Hear this Word" (3:1; 4:1; 5:1). Amos reminded the Jews of their unique privileges, that they only of all the families of the earth have been known by God. But privilege always entails responsibility: ". . . therefore, I will punish you for all your iniquities" (3:2). The remainder of chapter 3 spells out this fact. The next message is directed toward their sins, especially the insincerity of their formal religious ceremonies at Bethel and Gilgal (chapter 4). Amos' third message was an exhortation to turn to the Lord, for he was predicting the overthrow of the kingdom and the captivity (chapters 4, 5).

These messages were followed by a series of five visions, culminating with a view of the Lord standing upon the altar, ready to strike destruction with His own hand (chapters 7-9).

THE PROPHETIC MESSAGE

Looking beyond the captivity of Israel and their restoration to the land, Amos described that glorious era when Christ will come the second time.

> Behold, the days come, saith the Lord, that the plowman shall overtake the reaper, and the treader of grapes him that soweth seed; and the mountains shall drop sweet wine, and all the hills shall melt.
>
> And I will bring again the captivity of My people of Israel, and they shall build the waste cities, and inhabit them; and they shall plant vineyards, and drink their wine; they shall also make gardens, and eat the fruit of them.
>
> And I will plant them upon their land, and they shall no more be pulled up out of their land which I have given them, saith the Lord, thy God (Amos 9:13-15).

The apostle James quoted a part of this passage and revealed the divine purpose. God is now visiting the Gentiles "to take out of them a people for His name." Read the account in Acts 15. After the church has been called out (not the conversion of all the Gentiles but only the gathering out of an elect number), Christ will return. He will "build again the tabernacle of David, which is fallen down" (Acts 15:16). This He will do, restoring Israel to their land so "that the residue of men might seek after the Lord, and all the nations" (v. 17).

In the prophecy of Amos, as in the other books of the Old Testament, God's Son, the Lord Jesus Christ, is reflected in His glory and power.

OBADIAH

This little book is one of the shortest in the Bible. It is primarily a prophecy against Edom, a mountainous country southeast of Israel. It had been settled by the descendants of Esau, Jacob's brother. The people had been foes of Israel for centuries. Remember, it was Edom that refused Israel passage through their land on the way to Canaan. Because of this hostility, and because the prophet knew they would side with Israel's enemies, he delivered a scathing prophecy against Edom.

Prophecy is prewritten history. Obadiah knew that a foreign foe was coming. Esau was the son of Isaac just as Jacob was, but he cared more for the temporal things of the world than for his birthright (Genesis 25:27-34). His descendants were just like him. The message, therefore, is directed to those who have the opportunity to be spiritual but who choose instead to be worldly.

When Israel was hard-pressed, Edom refused to help them. They took a neutral stance; they adopted a do-nothing policy. Finally, they engaged in open hostility against Israel.

No personal history of the man Obadiah is given. We

do know that his name means "worshiper," or "servant of Jehovah." His writings foresee the doom of the Edomites. Although the Edomites have lost their national identity among the existing nations, God will search them out in the last days. Obadiah's prediction of the destruction about to befall them is a picture of the judgment to come upon the nations.

OUTLINE OF THE BOOK

    I. Doom upon Edom (vv. 1-9)
   II. The Cause for Destruction (vv. 10-14)
  III. The Day of the Lord (vv. 15-21)

STEPS IN EDOM'S DOWNFALL

Tracing the stages of Edom's decline is a valuable study. First, the prophet accused them of standing aloof (v. 11). In every conflict between right and wrong, the person who remains neutral does much of the damage. Second, they actually saw the destruction and distress of Jerusalem with their own eyes (v. 12). What a terrible thing to refuse to help the Lord's people! In the present Jewish situation, we would do well to consider the fact that God's attitude has not changed toward His chosen people. Oh, I know that one may argue the craftiness of the Jews, pointing out that they are still supplanters. Even so, we must not join those who would condemn them. I fear for any nation that causes grief to Israel. Third, the Edomites gloated when Israel fell (v. 12). Fourth, they spoke proudly; they had what we call the pharisaical attitude. Edom stood by and said, "That's all right; they probably deserved it." Fifth, not only were the Edomites guilty of wicked indifference, they eventually became actively involved in Israel's distress (v. 13). Sixth, Edom took advantage of Judah's trouble by plundering some of their wealth (v. 13). Sin is never the sudden outburst of a moment. (Note carefully the steps these relatives of Israel had taken in their downfall.) Seventh, they gave open assistance to the enemy (v. 14). When the Israelites escaped and tried to flee, the Edomites cut them off from their defenses and handed them over to their pursuers. Yes, it's the old story of the progression of sin. The Old Testament prophet was thundering out the New Testament principle of "whatever a man soweth, that shall he also reap" (Galatians 6:7).

Read verses 15 and 16 of Obadiah. Five years later Nebuchadnezzar invaded the mountain stronghold of Edom. The people learned the meaning of Obadiah's words, "As thou hast done, it shall be done unto thee; thy reward shall return upon thine own head" (v. 15).

The prophet used a familiar phrase which shows that the destruction of Edom was a type of further judgment to come at a later time. That phrase is "the day of the Lord."

THE LAST SCENE (vv. 15-21)

The Lord allowed the prophet to look beyond all judgments and to see Jehovah's ultimate triumph. This book, though brief, reaches forward to the second coming of the Lord Jesus. This prophecy promises both spiritual and national recovery to Israel and restoration to the scattered children of Jacob. It ends with this triumphant note: ". . . the kingdom shall be the Lord's" (v. 21). This is messianic. G. Campbell Morgan has said, "The final word of the prophecy is the final word of ALL prophecy, 'the kingdom shall be Jehovah's.'"

JONAH

The book of Jonah is different from the other minor prophets, for it's the personal experience of the prophet himself. The story is presented much like that of Elijah and Elisha. Though the book contains no direct prophecy, the experience of Jonah is itself a reflection of the message of God.

Jonah, whose name means "dove," was one of the earliest prophets. We know this from the book of 2 Kings, where a prediction of Jonah was fulfilled in the days of Jeroboam II (2 Kings 14:25).

A. C. Gaebelein has written, "The typical-prophetic meaning of the story of Jonah is authorized by the words of the Son of God. His experience typifies the death, the burial, and the resurrection of our Lord as well as the gospel message that goes forth to the Gentiles. Furthermore, Jonah's experience is prophetic also of the entire nation."

The Lord Jesus Christ Himself put His seal of authentication upon the story of Jonah (Matthew 12:40). Jonah was a man, not a myth; the book is fact, not fiction; it is history, not allegory.

OUTLINE OF THE BOOK
    I. Jonah Planning (1)
    II. Jonah Praying (2)

III. Jonah Preaching (3)
IV. Jonah Pouting (4)

JONAH PLANNING (chapter 1)

Jonah's name may indicate that he had a tender nature, but this tenderness was limited to his own people. He was a God-called, God-commissioned man with a God-given message. His sphere of service was as specific as his call. He was to go to Nineveh, the capital of Assyria, located on the banks of the Tigris River about 280 miles north of Babylon. The Assyrians were the fierce enemies of Israel.

Jonah tried to resign his commission and take a cruise on the Mediterranean. "He paid the fare," taking passage on a ship that was ready to sail to Tarshish (probably Spain). But the same Lord from whom he was trying to flee was preparing a wind to bring him to obedience. God's prophet was sleeping the sleep of self-complacency while the heathen sailors were about to perish. They were praying to their gods while Jonah was not even praying, just sleeping. When he was awakened, it took a series of humiliating questions to get him to confess. The conscience of those heathen men seemed to be more tender than that of the backslidden saint.

Jonah was finally cast into the sea. There a great fish was lying in wait. The Lord had prepared the huge creature to swallow the disobedient prophet.

JONAH PRAYING (chapter 2)

For 3 days and 3 nights Jonah was in the belly of the fish. There he began to pray. Had he prayed instead of fleeing from God, he would not have had this harrowing experience. Nevertheless his prayer was real. It had conviction, confession, contrition, and intercession. In his prayer he quoted from Psalms 18, 30, 31, 42, 69, 120, 130, and 142. In spite of his prayers, pledges, and vows, however, he was not delivered. It was not until Jonah confessed that "salvation is of the Lord," that God caused the fish to cast him upon the dry land.

JONAH PREACHING (chapter 3)

Although Jonah had gone through a traumatic experience and had reaffirmed his faith in God, he still needed to fulfill the Lord's commission to him. The Lord said again, "Arise, go unto Nineveh, that great city, and preach unto it the preaching that I bid thee" (3:2). Jonah did not hesitate this time. The consequence of his previous experience had made him obedient. He was now a God-called man with a God-given message on a God-directed mission.

Jonah delivered a message of repentance. To that city some 20 miles long and 12 miles wide, Jonah spoke the words the Lord had directed him to give. The Ninevites repented and believed God. We can well imagine what consternation this strange prophet caused as he cried, "Yet forty days, and Nineveh shall be overthrown" (v. 4). Jonah was learning a lesson that the apostle Paul later phrased in these words: "Is He the God of the Jews only? Is He not also of the Gentiles? Yes, of the Gentiles also" (Romans 3:29). God turned from His fierce anger, and Nineveh was spared, even though God knew that same city would later become the rod in His hand to chasten Israel.

JONAH POUTING (chapter 4)

How strange that this man of God was exceedingly displeased and grieved by the Lord's forbearance and patience with Nineveh. Jonah no doubt reasoned that the Assyrians would soon persecute his own people. But his displeasure was largely selfish. His own reputation as a prophet was at stake. He would rather witness the destruction of all the Assyrians than see himself dishonored. But God used a gourd to teach that poor, foolish servant a wonderful truth. Jonah was disgraced, and was forced to commit his reputation to the keeping of Jehovah. The prophet was more concerned about his own personal comfort than he was about the repentance and salvation of the inhabitants of that great city.

It is remarkable to trace the hand of God behind the

scenes of this story. It was God who sent out the wind. He prepared the fish, the gourd, the worm, and the east wind. No less remarkable is the fact that God took note of the little children in Nineveh—more than 120,000 of them—and even the cattle (4:11). What a contrast between the great loving heart of God and the narrow, selfish love of His reluctant and disobedient servant. The sinning saint is silenced, and God has the last word.

CHRIST IN THE BOOK

The great messianic picture reflected in Jonah is of the death, burial, and resurrection of the Lord Jesus. We are assured of this as we read these words of our Lord:

> An evil and adulterous generation seeketh after a sign, and there shall no sign be given to it, but the sign of the prophet, Jonah;
>
> For as Jonah was three days and three nights in the belly of the great fish, so shall the Son of man be three days and three nights in the heart of the earth (Matthew 12:39-41).

Dr. M. R. De Haan once said, "The miracle of Jonah consists in the fact that God raised him from the dead as a perfect type of our crucified, buried, and risen Lord." How appropriate are these words of the resurrected Christ to the two disciples on the road to Emmaus: "Ought not Christ to have suffered these things, and to enter into His glory? And beginning at Moses and all the prophets, He expounded unto them, in all the scriptures, the things concerning Himself" (Luke 24:26,27).

MICAH

Micah was a contemporary of Isaiah. Very little is said of the man except that he was a Morasthite, from a town near the Philistines. He prophesied in Judah, although his message mostly concerned Samaria. His cry was like that of a watchman upon the night air. He brought both the voice of warning and the voice of expectation.

OUTLINE OF THE BOOK

I. A Note of Warning (1)

The rapidly approaching doom of Samaria, the capital of the 10 tribes, is announced.

II. A Note of Wrath (2)

A cause of the overthrow is traced to the covetousness and worldliness of God's once highly favored people.

III. A Note of Threatening (3)

Princes and popular prophets are rebuked. Because of them, Jerusalem was to become rubble, and Zion would be plowed as a field.

IV. A Note of Promise (4)

When the Son of God appears, Jerusalem will shine in glory. Zion will become the meeting place for the millennial nations (v.1).

V. A Note of Announcement (5)

The place of Messiah's birth was prophesied (v. 2). He will become the peace of His people. He will deliver them from Antichrist, the Assyrian of the last days, and make the remnant of Jacob strong (a young lion) among the Gentiles.

VI. A Note of Instruction (6)

A tender pleading and upbraiding by Jehovah warns the children of Israel that they must suffer for their iniquities (v. 8).

VII. A Note of Hope (7)

In the midst of Jehovah's rebuke and indignation, the hope of the Lord's coming shines like a star in the dark sky. The prophecy closes with great joy and with eager anticipation of that day when God will cast Israel's sins into the depths of the sea.

PROPHECIES OF CHRIST

Few prophets have had more to say about the coming of Christ than Micah. We will consider some of the main elements.

1. *Micah Saw the Place of His Birth* (5:2). The "Highway of the Seed" begins in Genesis and continues through the Old Testament until Christ is born. In Genesis 3:15 we read of *the seed of the woman;* in Genesis 17, *of Abraham and his seed after him;* in Genesis 49:10, *of the tribe of Judah;* in 2 Samuel 7, *of the line of David;* and here in Micah 5:2, *Bethlehem Ephrathah.*

Many cities had this popular name, meaning "house of bread," but the prophet pinpointed it to be in Judah. Follow again the New Testament story about the way God fulfilled this promise by bringing Mary and Joseph to Bethlehem. When Herod asked the chief priests and scribes where Christ should be born, they quoted the words of Micah the prophet to him, "In Bethlehem of Judea; for thus it is written by the prophet, And thou Bethlehem, in the land of Judah, art not the least among the princes of Judah; for out of thee shall come a Governor that shall rule My people, Israel" (Matthew 2:5,6).

2. *Micah Saw His Humanity* (5:2). "Out of thee,"

168

Micah wrote. He did not say, out of heaven, though indeed that was where our Lord came from. But just like thousands of other men and women, He was born in Bethlehem. This One born in Bethlehem was to be "a ruler" over Israel. The Word was to be made flesh.

3. *Micah Saw His Deity* (5:2)". . . whose goings forth have been from of old, from everlasting." This is the same truth that Isaiah saw in chapter 9 of his prophecy, a truth that was later unfolded in the New Testament by Christ and the apostles:

"I and My Father are one" (John 10:30).

"Glorify Thou Me . . . with the glory which I had with Thee before the world was" (John 17:5).

"Before Abraham was, I am" (John 5:58).

"In the beginning was the Word, and the Word was with God, and the Word was God" (John 1:1).

"The Word was made flesh, and dwelt among us (and we beheld His glory . . .)" (John 1:14).

Micah saw the deity and humanity of Christ as few are privileged to see them.

4. *The Nature and Character of His Reign* (4:1-7). Peace will never be realized for our world until it is found in a person—and that person is the One of whom Micah spoke. He predicted:

a. Where the kingdom shall be established (4:2).

b. That the kingdom shall be supreme in power (see Daniel 7:13,14).

c. That the kingdom shall be peaceful (v. 3). What a day when nations will learn war no more!

d. That it will be a time of universal learning (v. 2). Discrediting the Word of God has been the cause of all the world's ills. It began in the garden of Eden and has continued to this present time. But a day is coming when there will be universal knowledge.

e. That universal prosperity will come (v. 4). The inequality in the present age will not diminish. We may talk of a "war on poverty," but poverty will never be abolished. Many of the ideals men are trying to bring about into this age really belong in the next.

f. That there will be universal worship (v. 5). The

prophet did not foresee the church. It was hidden from him. But he did look down the corridor of centuries to a time of universal worship in the kingdom. Another rendering of this verse may give a clearer meaning: "For all the people do now walk in the name of their god, but as for us, we shall walk in the name of the Lord, our God, forever and ever."

g. Who the ruler of the last days will be (vv. 6,7). The Lord of glory will put down rebellion and establish His righteous reign upon the earth. He taught His disciples to pray, "Thy kingdom come. Thy will be done in earth, as it is in heaven" (Matthew 6:10). This is the day of which Micah prophesied. Oh, what a day, when Christ reigns over this entire earth!

NAHUM

The book of Nahum is God's message of the impending destruction of Nineveh. The prophet's name means "comfort" or "consolation." He reminds us of Noah, whose name also means "rest," or "comfort." Nahum is the seventh chronologically of the minor prophets, and he ministered during the reign of Hezekiah.

About 150 years earlier, God had sent Jonah to deliver His warning to Nineveh. When the city repented, God held back His hand of judgment. Now "the burden of Nineveh" was laid upon Nahum's heart by God, and his prophecy graphically foretells the complete desolation of that people who oppressed the Jews. The destruction came 100 years later, when God in His holiness dealt harshly with the sin of Nineveh.

The great truths of the book of Nahum for believers today are its descriptions of God's character and power, for they depict the character and power of Jesus Christ. Few Old Testament books give us as much information on this subject as Nahum. The key verse of the prophecy is, "The Lord is slow to anger, and great in power, and will not at all acquit the wicked" (Nahum 1:3).

171

OUTLINE OF THE BOOK
I. Nineveh Judged (1)
II. Nineveh Sentenced (2)
III. Nineveh Executed (3)

Nineveh's destruction is minutely described, for Nahum wrote, "But with an overrunning flood He will make an utter end of the place, and darkness shall pursue His enemies" (1:8). Nineveh was beseiged by the Medes and the Babylonians. In the third year of that seige, the river was swollen with continual rains. It overflowed all of the city, breaking down the wall. The king built a large funeral pyre in the palace, collected all of his wealth, his concubines and eunuchs. He then burned the palace and everything in it, including himself and his servants. The enemy came in through the break in the wall and took the city.

1. *God controls the forces of nature* (1:3-5; 2:6). The prophet recognized that the God he worshiped was not a blind force. Nahum was not a pantheist. He believed that God is above nature and controls it; that God exists apart from matter. God has not wound up the universe, started it running, and then withdrawn from it. By Jesus Christ He has created all things, and the Son of God is the Sustainer of this universe. "For by Him were all things created, ... and He is before all things, and by Him all things consist [hold together]" (Colossians 1:16,17).

The same God that caused the wind to blow in Jonah's story would one day pick up the elements of nature and hurl them upon wicked Nineveh.

We have lost much of the Old Testament concept of God. A great tragedy may come into our midst and yet there is no repentance. An epidemic may sweep over the land, and yet no one turns to God. On every hand we see the works of the Lord in the affairs of men.

Little do we realize how much God has intervened in the control of this and other nations. The changing of the wind at the battle of Gettysburg turned the tide, sparing the union and eventually delivering the land from slavery. The psalmist declared, "He commandeth, and raiseth the stormy wind" (Psalm 107:25). Napoleon challenged the world and God, saying, "The Lord is on the side of the heaviest artillery." But it was the tiny snowflake that stopped his forward march and brought him to defeat. "Fire and hail; snow and vapor; stormy wind fulfilling His word" (Psalm 148:8).

A century after Nahum's prophecy, God turned loose His elements, and Nineveh fell to the armies of the Medes. The remains of that city were just a matter of conjecture until 1841, when the spade of the archeologist uncovered it and the Bible story was confirmed.

2. *God protects His own* (1:7). "The Lord is good, a stronghold in the day of trouble, and He knoweth those who trust in Him" (v. 7). What a wonderful verse! It stands like an island amid Nahum's troubled and tempest-tossed lake. All is calm, even though the context is a raging sea. Nahum is describing one of God's eternal attributes. The Lord Jesus said to the rich young ruler, "Why callest thou Me good? There is none good but one, that is, God" (Mark 10:18). Since Jesus Christ is God—God manifest in the flesh—He is good. He is good in Himself, essentially and independently. He is eternally and unchangeably good. The Father, Son, and Holy Spirit manifest this quality in every act of grace and providence. When is God good? In the day of trouble. "He knoweth those who trust in Him" (v. 7). "No good thing will He withhold from them who walk uprightly" (Psalm 84:11).

3. *He is a God of justice* (1:3). We learn in verse 3 that God "will not at all acquit the wicked." The mysteries of Calvary are bound up in that little phrase. Someone has written, "It put Jehovah to no test when He rolled shining stars from the palm of His creating hand and scooped out the channels for the tempestuous seas. But when it came to saving rebellious man, God faced that which tested the infinite." A holy God ordained just laws for the government of His world. Man broke the law. All men break it, and God indeed must judge them.

When a known criminal is pardoned, something is

desperately wrong with either the law or the administration of it. For God to show clemency to man would indicate the same flaw. Yet He is a God of mercy and love. How could He be just, and yet be the justifier of the sinner? The answer is found in the divine Substitute, the Lord Jesus Christ. John said, "Behold the Lamb of God!" (John 1:29). Here was One who was both an acceptable and "willing substitute."

Plato once said to Socrates, "God may forgive a deliberate sin, but I do not see how He can do it." I do! Some 300 years later the apostle John wrote, "The blood of Jesus Christ, His Son, cleanseth us from all sin" (1 John 1:7). The songwriter has written,

> I do not understand how it can be
> That even God could save a soul like me;
> But this I know, and in that surety hide,
> I only know that Christ the Savior died.

THE PROPHET'S VISION

Although he was burdened with the doom of the mighty city of Nineveh, Nahum closed chapter 1 with a word of consolation to the redeemed of the Lord. "Though I have afflicted thee, I will afflict thee no more. . . . Behold upon the mountains the feet of him that bringeth good tidings, that publisheth peace! O Judah, keep thy solemn feasts, perform thy vows; for the wicked shall no more pass through thee; he is utterly cut off" (1:12,15).

Like all of the prophets, Nahum looks forward to the time when Christ will come to reign in righteousness and justice. As in every other portion of the Old Testament Scriptures, the Lord's Anointed is visible upon the horizon. In Nahum we see both His character and His power, and we anticipate His glorious coming.

HABAKKUK

The prophet Habakkuk probably lived and proclaimed the message of God in the days of Josiah, the last king of Judah. We may assume this because Josiah observed the Passover and attempted to purify the temple. As Nahum had to bear the burden of Nineveh, so Habakkuk was chosen to bear the burden of Judah, who would soon fall to the Babylonians. These Chaldeans were to be used of God for the punishment of the Jews.

Habakkuk's prophecy, like that of Nahum, consists of three brief chapters. His name means "embracing." Not only did this name demonstrate his great love for God's people, but it also indicates that amid the gathering judgments he was safe in the embrace of God's love. Like most Old Testament prophets, Habakkuk saw judgment, dispersion, and future glory. The prophet's mind and message are centered upon Jehovah Himself.

OUTLINE OF THE BOOK
    I. The Prophet Pleads for Judah (1)
   II. God's Response: Judgment and Promise (2)
  III. The Prophet's Prayer and Song (3)

CHAPTER SUMMARIES

In Chapter 1, the announcement was made of the coming of the Chaldeans. Habakkuk earnestly entreated God to spare His people and deal justly with their enemies.

In Chapter 2, the prophet is in his watchtower, patiently waiting to hear how the Lord would respond to him. He learned that the vision was for an appointed time, "but at the end it shall speak, and not lie; though it tarry, wait for it, because it will surely come, it will not tarry" (v. 3). This promise reaches beyond Habakkuk's day and brings us to the close of this present dispensation. Then follow four woes upon Babylon (vv. 9,12,15,19). Babylon symbolizes the world's evil. But in the midst of this declaration of coming judgment is a wonderful promise that breaks out like sunshine through the storm: "For the earth shall be filled with the knowledge of the glory of the Lord, as the waters cover the sea" (v. 14).

In Chapter 3 are recorded a prayer and song of the prophet that take in the whole history of God's relationship with Israel. The book closes with a lofty expression of the confidence of faith (vv. 17,18).

THE PROPHET'S QUESTION

The keynote of faith rings throughout the entire prophecy. That resounding theme is introduced as follows: " . . . the just shall live by his faith" (2:4). This follows a dialog between Habakkuk and God, in which the prophet complained that God had permitted him to see only the iniquity of Israel (1:3). When Habakkuk learned that God was going to send the Chaldeans upon Judah as punishment for their sins, he challenged God. He asked why the Lord would use that heathen nation when they were so much more wicked than God's covenant people. In fact, Habakkuk raised one of the common questions of the ages, "Thou art of purer eyes than to behold evil, and canst not look on iniquity; why lookest Thou upon them that deal treacherously, and holdest Thy tongue when the wicked devoureth the man that is more righteous than he?" (1:13). Much the same attitude was expressed by the psalmist when he wrote, "For I was envious of the foolish, when I saw the prosperity of the wicked" (Psalm 73:3).

You and I must admit that the earth is filled with glaring inequity. The wicked *do* seem to prosper while the righteous suffer. And I'm sure you've asked the same question, perhaps in a different way.

GOD'S ANSWER

We should pay close attention to the answer God gave the prophet Habakkuk. It will help make us better Christians, better servants of the Lord, and less inclined to complaining. Observe that Jehovah's answer began with the command to "write the vision." The world needs this message; preserve it. " . . . make it plain upon tablets" (2:2); that is, carve it in stone, put it on the signposts so that every passerby can read it. In essence, Jehovah was saying that He wanted everyone to know His answer to the prophet's question.

The first thing we learn is that God is running things on schedule (2:3). Our time and God's time are not measured on the same dial. For centuries Israel had to offer sacrifices for sins. They pointed toward Christ, the coming sacrifice for sins. But Israel became tired and lapsed into idolatry. Yet "when the fullness of the time was come, God sent forth His Son" (Galatians 4:4). You can count on it—not a single promise will fail! A thousand years are as a day in God's sight.

These truths are steppingstones to the theme verse of the book (2:4). It is God's answer to all the questions of Habakkuk, and it's His answer to the questions of our own souls as well. It's expressed in the words, "The just shall live by his faith" (Habakkuk 2:4).

That great statement made by Jehovah to Habakkuk is repeated three times in the New Testament. All three express an aspect of the sufficient work of Christ on behalf of the believer. Although the truth is developed in the New Testament, the seedplot is in the Old, here in Habakkuk. We will benefit from a brief look at the three places the statement appears in the New Testament.

1. *Romans 1:17.* This verse follows the well-known statement of the apostle, "For I am not ashamed of the gospel of Christ" (1:16). Paul continued, "For in it is the righteousness of God revealed from faith to faith; as it is written, The just shall live by faith" (v. 17). The apostle is standing on the threshold of the great epistle of justification. This doctrine includes not only the wiping away of the believing sinner's guilt and the penalty of sin, but also the placing of the believer in a righteous position before God. God has left us a record, the Bible, telling us what He has done. By faith we accept it. This is the initial step in the pathway of belief. Abel is the first example of this, because the Scripture says, "By faith Abel offered unto God a more excellent sacrifice than Cain, by which he obtained witness that he was righteous" (Hebrews 11:4).

2. *Galatians 3:11.* The next use of these words from Habakkuk is as follows: "But that no man is justified by the law in the sight of God, it is evident; for, The just shall live by faith" (Galatians 3:11). Why did the apostle Paul use this quotation in writing to the Galatian Christians? Well, they had begun by faith. Paul had preached; they had believed. But now they were tempted to go back to the works of the law as a principle of the Christian walk. The apostle therefore showed them that just as they were saved by faith, they were to walk by faith. This is how Abraham "looked for a city whose builder and maker is God" (Hebrews 11:10) and did not know the place he was going (v. 8). In addition, he did not know how the seed was to be born (v. 11). Nor did he know why Isaac would be offered and then raised (v. 17). All of this speaks of the walk of faith.

3. *Hebrews 10:38.* This quotation of the verse from Habakkuk appears in the context of scriptural teaching about the believer's assurance. When the night is blackest, faith pierces the darkness and sees the coming of morning.

We are justified by faith; we walk by faith; we will

178

be delivered by faith. This is the vision God gave the prophet of old. He let His servant know that He was working out His eternal purposes; He lets us know too. Here is a promise for our faith to rest upon: "For the earth shall be filled with the knowledge of the glory of the Lord, as the waters cover the sea" (Habakkuk 2:14).

As in previous books of the Old Testament, the name "LORD" is the name "Jehovah." This is the covenant-keeping God of redemption; it's the Lord Jesus Christ. Habakkuk's own faith shone through the shadows of great trial, and this song welled up within his heart: "Yet I will rejoice in the Lord, I will joy in the God of my salvation" (3:18). Who is the "God of salvation"? "Thou shalt call His name Jesus; for He shall save His people from their sins" (Matthew 1:21).

ZEPHANIAH

Zephaniah prophesied during the time of Josiah, a time of temporary revival. He saw the dark clouds of apostasy and judgment creeping over the horizon. The book of 2 Kings, chapter 22, gives the historical background of this period. Zephaniah has been called the "compendium of prophecy." He saw the judgment that was soon to fall upon Israel for her apostasy. Then he looked down the ages to the judgment of the whole earth. And beyond that he envisioned the time of universal blessing to follow. We read one phrase repeatedly in Zephaniah's prophecy: "The day of the Lord."

Habakkuk stood high and looked far; Zephaniah stooped low with the candle of searching and looked closely.

OUTLINE OF THE BOOK

I. The Day of the Lord (1:1-2:3)

The prophet describes the day of God's wrath, which will be fulfilled in the coming invasion and captivity of Israel. It foreshadows the final day of the Lord.

II. Judgment upon the Nations (2:4-15)

The prophet predicts an outpouring of God's wrath

upon certain peoples and nations. Read the history books and you will find that these have been fulfilled in minute detail.

III. Israel's Sinfulness (3:1-7)

The terrible moral state of Israel is described. This is what called for and justified the judgment that was about to fall.

IV. The Kingdom Described (3:8-20)

This passage presents an interesting glimpse of the millennial period and the blessings Israel will experience during that time.

The iniquity of the inhabitants of Judah and Jerusalem weighed heavily upon the heart of Zephaniah. He was a contemporary of Jeremiah, who was called the "weeping prophet."

In verse 2 of chapter 3, Zephaniah named the four sins that cursed Israel. We will see that each was a sin of omission.

1. *She obeyed not the voice.* What marvelous privileges the Israelites enjoyed! No other people had received such recognition from God. Elijah had come with the message of Jehovah; Elisha had followed him. Prophet after prophet had appeared with fresh pronouncements from the courts of glory. But Israel would not listen to the voice of the Lord.

2. *She received not correction.* The Jews did not seem to understand why God had allowed the heathen kingdoms to come and plague them. Read again the book of Judges and the history recorded in Samuel, Kings, and Chronicles. The record of judgment occurs over and over again. And yet the people would not learn.

3. *She trusted not in the Lord.* The Israelites were relying upon something other than their God. When war was impending, they made alliances with other nations rather than trusting Jehovah. Although these other nations worshiped false gods, Israel compromised by joining forces with them. As a result, idolatry soon was being practiced by God's people.

4. *She drew not near to her God.* The people had no fellowship with the Almighty. The altars were torn down

and the sacrifices stopped. They had knowledge but no spirit.

What was the remedy for all of this? Divine judgment! And the judgments proclaimed by Zephaniah are forerunners of future judgments. Like the prophet Joel, Zephaniah spoke of the day of the Lord. In fact, just preceding the universal judgment that will come upon this earth in the endtime, worldwide conditions will be similar to those local conditions in Israel. The inevitable result is given as follows:

Therefore, wait upon Me, saith the Lord, until the day that I rise up to the prey; for My determination is to gather the nations, that I may assemble the kingdoms, to pour upon them Mine indignation, even all My fierce anger; for all the earth shall be devoured with the fire of My jealousy (Zephaniah 3:8).

But while these judgments are sweeping the scene of the world's defilement, a remnant will be spared. They are described by Zephaniah as "an afflicted and poor people." Of them it is said, "And they shall trust in the name of the Lord" (3:12).

This believing remnant will form the nucleus of a saved and restored people at the second coming of Christ. No wonder the prophecy of Zephaniah ends with such a beautiful promise about this remnant of Israel!

Sing, O daughter of Zion; shout, O Israel; be glad and rejoice with all the heart, O daughter of Jerusalem ....

The Lord, thy God, in the midst of thee is mighty; He will save, He will rejoice over thee with joy; He will rest in His love; He will joy over thee with singing ....

Behold, at that time I will undo all that afflict thee; and I will save her that is lame, and gather her that was driven out; and I will get them praise and fame in every land where they have been put to shame.

At that time will I bring you again, even in the

time that I gather you; for I will make you a name
and a praise among all peoples of the earth, when I
turn back your captivity before your eyes, saith the
Lord (Zephaniah 3:14,17,19,20).

Tell me, who is it that is going to perform this marvelous work in behalf of Israel? None other than the One
whose right it is to reign—God's anointed—the Lord
Jesus. The exhortation of Peter in his second epistle
seems appropriate,

Seeing, then, that all these things shall be dissolved,
what manner of persons ought ye to be in all holy
living and godliness,

Looking for and hasting unto the coming of the
day of God, in which the heavens, being on fire, shall
be dissolved, and the elements shall melt with
fervent heat? (2 Peter 3:11,12).

HAGGAI

This prophet, whose name means "festive" or "festival of the Lord," was the first of the post-exile prophets. About 50,000 Jews had come back from Babylon after 70 years of captivity. The task before these people was the rebuilding of the wall and city of Jerusalem, the restoration of the temple, and the reviving of its religious activities.

In spite of the noble endeavor before them, they soon forgot the Lord. As the book of Haggai begins, 15 months have already elapsed since their return. The temple remains in ruins, and no one has attempted to repair it. Jehovah therefore raised up two prophets, Haggai and Zechariah, so that His name and His house might not be kept in dishonor.

Haggai was the first of these prophets. He is called "Jehovah's messenger." Although his style was plain and his language simple, God placed upon him the high honor of being His spokesman.

Haggai preached four sermons to this returned remnant during a period of three months. They give us the structure of the book.

OUTLINE OF THE BOOK

    I. The Neglect of God's House (1)
    II. The Problem of Dissatisfaction (2:1-9)

184

III. Moral Conditions in Jerusalem (2:10-19)
IV. Future Judgment and Glory (2:20-23)

THE NEGLECT OF GOD'S HOUSE

Haggai's initial sermon was delivered on the first day of September, 520 B.C. He appealed to the people's sense of shame. God's house was in ruins while they lived in comfortable homes. They had shamefully neglected the house of the Lord. You may excuse them, saying, "They had been there only a few months." The Bible clearly tells us, however, to seek "*first* the kingdom of God, and His righteousness" (Matthew 6:33).

What bearing does Haggai's message have on us today? Paul said in Romans 15:4, "For whatever things were written in earlier times were written for our learning." It is impossible to ignore God and His interests without reaping the consequences. The people had sowed very little and were reaping little. They ate, but they were not filled. They drank, but they were not satisfied. They put on clothes, but they were not warm. They received wages for their labor, but they had a hole in their pocketbooks. They gathered wood, but God's breath of judgment was upon it. As a result, the dew from heaven had been withheld, and the fields that produced their food had failed (1:6).

The intervention of God is strikingly expressed in verse 11, "And I called for a drought upon the land, upon the mountains, and upon the grain, and upon the new wine, and upon the oil, and upon that which the ground bringeth forth, and upon men, and upon cattle, and upon all the labor of the hands." The Jews had put God and His work in second place, and had given priority to themselves. God had responded in judgment.

Haggai's sermon was effective, for we learn that the temple was soon repaired (1:14).

DISSATISFACTION

This produced the need for Haggai's second sermon. The people had worked hard on the temple and finished it. But the restored temple was not nearly as good or as beautiful or as grand as the old temple. The prophet ob-

185

served, "Is it not in your eyes in comparison with it as nothing?" (2:3). The Jews were comparing the present with the past. The prophet had a message from God for the complainers, and it had four parts:

1. Jehovah said, "I am with you" (v. 4).
2. Jehovah gave the assurance of His presence (v. 5).
3. God predicted that He would "shake all nations" (v. 7).
4. God promised that the glory of the heavenly temple would be much greater than the one they were weeping over (v. 9).

MORAL CONDITIONS OF ISRAEL

The picture Haggai gave was taken from the law of Moses. It referred to the regulation Jehovah had given to His people Israel about touching a dead body, thus producing ceremonial uncleanness (Haggai 2:11-13). The prophet applied it to the people of his day, saying, "So is this people, and so is this nation before Me, saith the Lord" (v. 14). Their hearts were wrong. Haggai was given the spiritual perception to see that the neglect of the Lord's house and the terrible complaining had come from within. Nothing that the people could do would be pleasing to God until they established a right heart condition. They could not see this, however, even though God's stern hand of judgment had come upon them. The moral condition of the Jews in that day pictures the moral degradation of the days in which we are living.

FUTURE JUDGMENT AND GLORY

On the same day he gave his third message, the prophet delivered still another sermon. But this time he spanned the ages and declared the word of the Lord concerning the endtime (2:20-23). We know that he leaped the centuries and saw the future, because the inspired penman of the epistle to the Hebrews quoted Haggai's prophecy as follows: "Whose voice then shook the earth; but now He hath promised, saying, Yet once more I shake not the earth only, but also heaven" (Hebrews 12:26). The book of Hebrews gave the same warning to the church in this age that Haggai gave to the Jews.

What will this day of judgment be like? It will mean the overturning of the nations, for the age will end in terrible conflict (see Revelation 19:17-20). Following this, God's chosen One will sit on the throne of His glory and rule in peace and righteousness. Zerubbabel became a type of the Lord Jesus Christ in this respect, for the Lord said to him through Haggai, "I . . . will make thee as a signet; for I have chosen thee" (Haggai 2:23). Zerubbabel therefore is a reflection of Christ in His princely office.

The words of Psalm 2 are echoed at the conclusion of Haggai's prophecy: "Yet have I set My king upon My holy hill of Zion. I will declare the decree: The Lord hath said unto Me, Thou art My Son; this day have I begotten Thee. Ask of Me, and I shall give Thee the nations for Thine inheritance, and the uttermost parts of the earth for Thy possession" (Psalm 2:6-8). In Acts 13, the apostle Paul in the synagogue at Antioch quoted these words, declaring to all that they refer to the Lord Jesus Christ.

ZECHARIAH

The book of Zechariah has often been called the "Revelation" of the Old Testament. The 14 chapters are largely given over to prophetic symbols of the future. The historical setting of the book is identical with that of Haggai. Zechariah is concerned almost exclusively with the Jew and the Messiah. Haggai was written chiefly with the temple and the religious state of God's ancient people in mind, but Zechariah took a broader view. He unfolded the future of Israel and the Gentile nations to the second coming of the Lord Jesus Christ and the establishment of His millennial kingdom.

The church is not pictured in Zechariah. Looking down through the centuries, the prophet saw the humility and glory of Messiah, but he did not see the time between the first and second comings of Christ.

OUTLINE OF THE BOOK

    I.   Eight Visions about Israel's Future (1-6)

    II.   Detailed Prophecies of the Endtime (7-14)

It's impossible in one brief chapter to explain all the various symbols in this book. In the first six chapters, the prophet recorded eight visions he had seen—all of them about Israel.

1. A rider on a red horse among the myrtle trees depicts Israel in dispersion but not forgotten (1:7-11).

2. Four horns, which are four world empires that have scattered Israel (1:18,19).

3. Four carpenters, which represent the destruction of Gentile supremacy (1:20,21).

4. A man with a measuring line, showing Israel's future prosperity (2:1-3).

5. Joshua before the Lord, Satan accusing, and a picture of Israel cleansed and restored (3).

6. The candlestick, a picture of Israel as God's light-bearer (4:1-7).

7. The flying roll, illustrating the reign of divine law on the earth (5:1-4).

8. Four chariots, speaking of judgment upon the earth (6:1-8).

The remnant had returned to Jerusalem, but it was only a handful compared to the days before the captivity. They were discouraged, and they needed a message from God. These visions were given to the prophet to encourage Israel in one of her darkest hours.

Chapter 8 of Zechariah closes with one of the most remarkable statements in all of Scripture. "Thus saith the Lord of hosts: In those days it shall come to pass that ten men shall take hold out of all languages of the nations, even shall take hold of the skirt of him that is a Jew, saying, We will go with you; for we have heard that God is with you" (v. 23). How different from the experience of Israel through the centuries! Knowing that a time like this would come should have given great encouragement to God's people in the land.

VISIONS OF THE ENDTIME

Second only to Isaiah, the prophet Zechariah gives us one of the most complete pictures of the Messiah in the Old Testament. Look at what he foresaw.

1. *The humility of Israel's Messiah* (9:9). What a peculiar prediction this was! That Israel's king was coming was neither peculiar nor a surprise; it was the expectation of the nation, for the prophets had spoken of it. But

the Jews were looking for Him in gorgeous array, with dashing steeds and golden chariots, perhaps coming down from heaven. Zechariah, however, predicted that He would come "lowly, and riding upon an ass, and upon a colt, the foal of an ass" (9:9).

Half a millennium had passed before the Lord Jesus said to His disciples one day, "Go into the village opposite you, in which, at your entering, you shall find a colt tied, on which yet never man sat; loose him, and bring him here" (Luke 19:30). Christ entered Jerusalem amid the plaudits of the crowd, riding upon a colt in exact fulfillment of prophecy. Oh, the accuracy of the minute details in the Word! What other book would dare risk such predictions?

2. *He foresaw His betrayal* (11:12,13). How Zechariah must have pondered these words, expressed centuries later by Judas! The prophet probably could not understand. Peter told us that "the prophets have inquired and searched diligently, who prophesied of the grace that should come unto you, searching what, or what manner of time the Spirit of Christ who was in them did signify, when He testified beforehand the sufferings of Christ, and the glory that should follow" (1 Peter 1:10,11). Zechariah recorded, "So they weighed for My price thirty pieces of silver" (v. 12). That was the price of a slave. If an ox gored a slave, the owner of the ox had to pay the slave owner 30 pieces of silver. Our Lord took the place of a slave. The word "redemption" means "to deliver by paying a price." This prophecy is quoted in Matthew 27:9,10 when Judas betrayed Jesus for 30 pieces of silver, and when the chief priest took that silver and bought the potter's field, a place of burial.

3. *Zechariah portrayed scenes from the night of Christ's betrayal* (13:7). "Awake, O sword, against My shepherd, and against the man who is My fellow, saith the Lord of hosts; smite the shepherd, the sheep shall be scattered; and I will turn Mine hand upon the little ones." The fulfillment is recorded in the gospel of Matthew. The disciples were with Jesus on the Mount of Olives when He said, "All ye shall be offended because of Me this night;

190

for it is written, I will smite the shepherd, and the sheep of the flock shall be scattered abroad" (26:31). "Then they spat in His face, and buffeted Him; and others smote Him with the palms of their hands" (26:67). When Jesus spoke of that awful hour (v. 31), He harked back 500 years to this prophecy. The shepherd is the same as described in Zechariah 11:4-14.

The word used for "fellow" in Zechariah 13:7 is the word *amithi.* The only other place it appears is in Leviticus, where it refers to laws about injuries inflicted upon close relatives. It is used interchangeably with the word "brother." Zechariah uses it here to refer to the Messiah, who is connected with God in His very essence. "No man hath seen God at any time; the only begotten Son, who is in the bosom of the Father, He hath declared Him" (John 1:18). When the Lord Jesus said, "I and My Father are one," the Jews took up stones to stone Him. This One to whom Zechariah referred could only be the Son of God.

4. *Zechariah foresaw the main events related to the second coming.* He saw Israel regathered and the tribulation period. He presented the scene in the first 9 verses of chapter 12. "Behold, I will make Jerusalem a cup of trembling unto all the peoples round about..." (v. 2). "And in that day will I make Jerusalem a burdensome stone" (v. 3). "... all the nations of the earth [will] be gathered together against it" (v. 3). "Jerusalem shall be inhabited again in her own place" (v. 6). "The Lord also shall save the tents of Judah first..." (v. 7). "In that day shall the Lord defend the inhabitants of Jerusalem" (v. 8). "And it shall come to pass, in that day, that I will seek to destroy all the nations that come against Jerusalem" (v. 9). Chapter 14 begins with the climactic events that lead to the return of Christ.

Zechariah was given prophetic insight concerning Israel's repentance. Chapter 12, verse 10, declares, "And I will pour upon the house of David, and upon the inhabitants of Jerusalem, the Spirit of grace and of supplications; and they shall look upon Me whom they have pierced, and they shall mourn for Him, as one mourneth for his only son, and shall be in bitterness for Him, as one that is in bitterness for his firstborn."

Zechariah graphically portrayed God's judgment upon the nations at the battle of Armageddon. Verses 12 through 15 of chapter 14 speak of "the plague with which the Lord will smite all the peoples that have fought against Jerusalem."

If Zechariah were not writing under inspiration, his predictions would be those of a fool. But, borne along by the Holy Spirit, he was speaking of Christ's millennial reign when he said, "And the Lord shall be king over all the earth; in that day shall there be one Lord, and His name one" (14:9). Jerusalem will be the center of our Lord's reign over this earth.

What a scene of peace, tranquillity, and holiness is described in the closing verses of this prophecy! Zechariah wrote, "And it shall come to pass that every one that is left of all the nations which came against Jerusalem shall even go up from year to year to worship the King, the Lord of hosts, and to keep the feast of tabernacles" (Zechariah 14:16). The prophecy of Zechariah is filled with references to Jehovah, the Lord Jesus Christ. Our Lord Himself said, "They spoke of Me."

MALACHI

With the prophecy of Malachi, God brought to a close the Old Testament revelation of Himself to His chosen people Israel. For more than 400 years the heavens would be silent until the stern voice of John the Baptist would thunder the message of repentance in preparation for the coming of the Messiah. Israel would suffer much during those years, and a look at Malachi will reveal the cause of that suffering.

This concludes our study of how Christ is reflected in the 39 books of the Old Testament. "Malachi" means "the messenger of the Lord." His prophecy deals with the sad spiritual condition of Israel. He wrote in the period following the days of Haggai and Zechariah, an era which corresponds in so many ways with the close of this present age because of coldness toward God and professionalism among the spiritual leaders. We must remember that man—wherever he is placed and however hard he may try to lift himself up—is a wretched failure. Then, as now, the masses of the people were "lovers of pleasures more than lovers of God, having a form of godliness, but denying the power of it" (2 Timothy 3:4,5).

The prophecy of Malachi was given shortly after the time of Nehemiah. Read the book of Nehemiah and you will find the setting of this prophecy and this threefold description of the corruption in Israel:

1. The priesthood defiled (Nehemiah 13:7-9,29).

2. The nation had an idolatrous alliance with the heathen nations around them (Nehemiah 13:23,24). This resulted in the mixed language.

3. The support of the house of God was neglected (Nehemiah 13:10-12). The Levites were not given their inheritance by the people of Israel. They looked after the temple service and were to be supported by the tithe. But they were working in the fields to provide for themselves, and the house of God was neglected.

At the time when these deplorable conditions prevailed in Israel, God raised up Malachi. He soon began to hurl maledictions at Israel for her sins. Some thought the prophet was old-fashioned; others said he was a troublemaker; still others thought he should keep quiet.

The sad part of the story of Malachi is that the people were not aware of their awful condition. This is noted in seven questions the Jews asked throughout the prophecy. We will look at them more carefully.

SEVEN QUESTIONS OF THE PEOPLE

1. *In what way hast Thou loved us?* (1:2). Israel was almost insolent in asking this question. They were so blind that they could not see any indications that God was displaying His love. All Jehovah had to do was ask them to compare themselves with their neighbor Edom, the descendants of Esau. God had not shown His particular favor to Esau and his descendants but to Jacob and his children. The fact that Israel failed to see this illustrates the blinding effect of sin.

2. *In what way have we despised Thy name?* (1:6). Jehovah reminded the Israelites that a son honors his father and a servant honors his master, but that they had no fear of Him in their hearts. How much like today! People profess to be the children of God, but they do not act like it. Their very demeanor indicates that they are bringing disgrace to His name.

3. *In what way have we polluted Thee?* (1:7). They had been offering animals that were lame and sick and blind for sacrifice. They offered the most contemptible things to their great Creator and Provider. No human governor would ever tolerate such action. Men would not even treat their employer like Israel was treating God. Malachi's words to Israel are certainly applicable to professing Christians today.

4. *In what way have we wearied Him?* (2:17). Note the context of this question. It has to do primarily with family life, and particularly with the marriage relationship. "For the Lord, the God of Israel, saith that He hateth putting away" (v. 16). The prophet speaks of the judgment that will fall because of this, but the people don't believe it. They don't think God is keeping track. They say, "Where is the God of justice?" (v. 17). Considering the plague of divorce that is sweeping our land, even in Christian circles, how do we dare think we can escape the chastening hand of God?

5. *In what way shall we return?* (3:7). Their attitude suggests that they did not even know they had strayed from the Lord. Israel actually thought they were doing God a service. How many today mumble through some prayer, make their declaration of church membership, and speak vaguely of some previous experience, but are not aware that they are far away from God!

6. *How have we robbed Thee?* (3:8). "Will a man rob God?" It is almost as if they respond, "Preposterous! A man will not even rob a fellowman." But God said, "Ye have robbed Me" in tithes and offerings.

7. *What have we spoken so much against Thee?* (3:13). The context in verse 14 indicates that they had spoken against the Lord in both word and action. Oh, they had kept up their religious ceremonies but were not worshiping God in their hearts. All the while they were bringing torn, lame animals for sacrifice. And they were trying to outdo each other in making money, procuring divorces, and indulging their lusts.

THE FAITHFUL REMNANT

In the midst of all these people with an empty profession of faith was a little remnant that feared the Lord. They "spoke often one to another; and the Lord hearkened, and heard it, and a book of remembrance was written before Him for them that feared the Lord, and that thought upon His name" (Malachi 3:16).

Then Malachi leaped the centuries and saw the time when men shall be rewarded. A remnant of Israel, the "hidden treasure" of Matthew 13, will experience the fulfillment of Jehovah's words: "And they shall be Mine, saith the Lord of hosts, in that day when I make up My jewels; and I will spare them, as a man spareth his own son that serveth him" (Malachi 3:17).

Chapter 4 of Malachi speaks of that day of judgment when the proud and the wicked shall be like stubble. But to those who fear His name, the appearing Christ will be the "Sun of righteousness" (v. 2), arising with healing in His wings.

Thus the Old Testament canon is brought to a close. In every book the person and work of the Lord Jesus is reflected, pointing forward to His incarnation, His perfect life, His sacrificial death for our sins, His victorious resurrection, and His glorious return to defeat Satan, to purge the world of evil, and to establish His kingdom of righteousness and peace. We have seen the One of whom it is written, "It pleased the Father that in Him should all fullness dwell" (Colossians 1:19).

Reflections of Christ in the Old Testament

As you continue your study of God's Word, you will no doubt discover additional pictures of Christ. Use these pages to record them for later reference and study.

Christ in the Pentateuch

Christ in the
Historical Books

Christ in the Poetical Books

Christ in the
Prophetical Books